현장 속에서 배우는 생생한

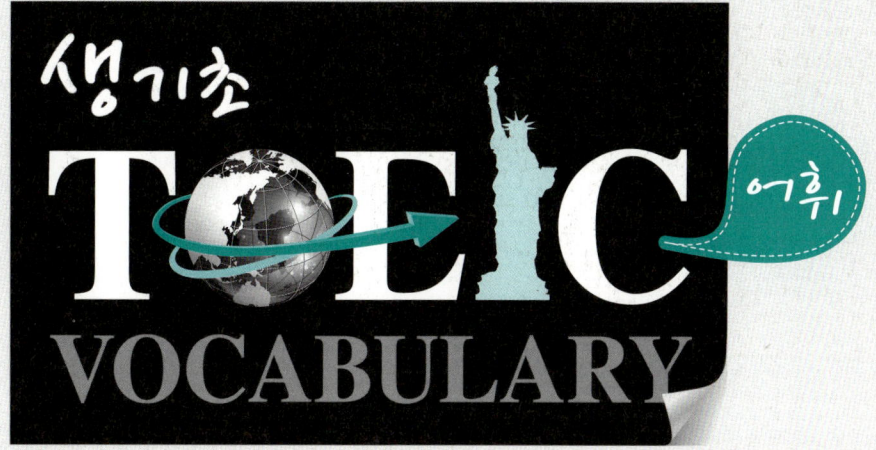

생기초

TOEIC
VOCABULARY

어휘

Preface

생기초 토익 어휘!
가장 빈도 높은 상황 별 토익 어휘 정복!!!

이 책은 TOEIC 점수 향상을 목표로 하는 350–700점 사이의 초급, 중급자를 대상으로, 토익에서 빈도 수가 높게 출제되는 상황들을 중심으로 전개되는 영어 회화와 그 상황에 연계되는 TOEIC 단어/표현 파트를 융합함으로써 토익의 기본 실력을 배양할 수 있도록 기획되었습니다. 토익 관련 서적의 홍수 속에서 차별화되는 이 책의 특징은 무엇일까요?

집필 목적은?

이 책은 기존의 단순 문제 풀이 식 강의라거나 문맥이 결핍된 독립 단어만을 학습하는 전통적인 단순 암기 방식을 지양하며, 학습자는 상황 맥락 속에서 지문 속에 응축된 어휘를 학습하게 됩니다. 즉, 우리는 이 책에서 Yuna라는 주인공과 함께 길 찾기, 공항 통과하기, 벼룩시장 물건 흥정하기, 은행 계좌 열기, 인터넷 영화 예매하기, 생일 파티 하기 등의 구체적 상황을 몸으로 부딪혀 학습하는 능력을 함양할 수 있도록 하는 데 초점을 두었습니다.

또한, 학습자의 자발적인 참여를 위해 음성 녹음 및 확인 활동, 퀴즈, 발음 비교, 롤 플레이 등의 기능을 포함하여 학습자 중심의 수준별 반복 학습을 가능하도록 하여 말하기, 쓰기, 독해, 어휘 등의 다양한 언어 기능을 통합적으로 향상시키는 것을 목표로 합니다.

흥미로운 에듀테인먼트(edutainment)와 접목시켰다

이 교재는 드라마적 구성을 채택하고 있어 주인공을 중심으로 상황에 따른 표현을 익히는 회화 연습을 할 수 있습니다. 또한 독자로 하여금 공부와 흥미 두 마리 토끼를 모두 잡을 수 있도록 대화, 사진, 그림 등을 다양하게 활용해 과학적이고 인지–감각적인 학습을 가능하게 하였습니다.

21세기 영어 어휘 학습의 신경향을 반영했다

연어(collocation), 덩어리 표현(chunk), 구 표현(phraseology) 등을 포괄적으로 활용한 21세기 단어 학습법을 통해 원어민과 같은 유창한 표현을 익힐 수 있습니다.

Whole Language로 접근하였다

TOEIC 어휘 학습뿐 아니라 회화, 청취, 독해 등 다양한 방법을 통해 영어의 다기능을 총체적(whole language)으로 향상시킵니다.

온라인 강의로도 즐길 수 있다

최고의 온라인 교육 환경을 제공하는 CUFS(사이버한국외국어대학교)(www.cufs.ac.kr)에서 첨단의 기술로 제작된 강의를 통해 반복적인 학습이 가능합니다. 또한 21세기 독자가 원하는 방향에 발맞춰 트위터, 블로그 등을 통해 독자와의 소통이 이루어지도록 하여 최상의 학습 효과를 낼 수 있도록 도와줍니다.

마지막으로 늘 사랑과 지원을 보내주신 사이버 한국외국어대학교의 학우들과 교수님들, 가족 그리고 박수아, 주성은, 한정원 튜터에게 감사의 말을 전합니다.

2012년

김희진

Contents

현장 속에서 배우는 생생한

생기초
TOEIC 어휘
VOCABULARY

I am books

Chapter 01

Preparing to Go Abroad

| **Topic** | Preparing to Go Abroad |
| **Summary** | Mike and Yuna are going to be moved to an overseas branch. Their supervisor Mr. Smith comes to give them the good news. |

| **주제** | 해외 발령 준비 |
| **줄거리** | 마이크와 유나는 해외 지사로 가게 된다. 그들의 상사인 스미스씨는 좋은 소식을 전하러 그들에게 온다. |

Pre-check Quiz ✳

Q. 다음 중 의미 설명이 틀린 것을 고르시오.

a. overseas branch – 해변가의 사무소

b. application – 지원서

c. International driver's license – 국제 운전면허증

d. for starters – 우선

🎧 Dialogue ✳

Yuna	Mike, I heard your job application for the US branch has been accepted.
Mike	You did? Did Mr. Smith tell you that?
Yuna	No, I overheard him. Oh, speak of the devil — here he comes.
Smith	Congratulations! You are both being transferred to the overseas branch.
Yuna	Wow, I got the spot! What am I going to need?
Smith	For starters, a passport, a working visa and an international driver's license.

- -

유나	마이크, 네 미국 지사 발령지원서가 수락됐다는 소식을 들었어.
마이크	들었어? 스미스 상사님이 말씀해 주셨니?
유나	아니, 그분의 말씀을 엿들었어. 호랑이도 제 말 하면 온다고, 지금 오시네.
스미스	축하해! 너희들 둘 다 해외 지사로 발령됐어.
유나	우와, 나도 가게 되었네! 무엇이 필요할까?
스미스	우선, 여권, 워킹 비자와 국제 운전면허증이 필요해.

01 Comprehension Questions

1. Who is moving to New York?

   a. only Yuna   b. only Mike

   c. Mr. Smith   d. Yuna and Mike

   HINT You are *both* being transferred to the overseas branch.

2. What is not an item Yuna and Mike need to prepare?

   a. passport   b. a visa that permits employment

   c. international credit card   d. driving certification

   HINT For starters, a passport, a working visa and an international driver's license.

02 Vocabulary

1. Visa (working, tourist, etc) : (취업, 관광) 비자

   어원 라틴어의 vise(비자) : '보증하다' → 발행 나라 입국 자유 보증 권리

2. International driver's license : 국제 운전면허증

   ↔ domestic driver's license

3. overseas branch : 해외 지점

   가지 → 분파 → 지점/점포 + overseas

4. application : 신청 → 적용/응용 → 지원서

   Your job application for the US branch has been accepted.

5. transfer : 이동시키다/옮기다 → 발령 + overseas

   You are both being transferred to the overseas branch.

6. for starters : 우선, 시작

   For starters, I will have broccoli soup.

1. **I got the spot.** 내가 그 자리(직책)를 맡게 되었어.

   ▪ **표현설명**

   spot   ⓝ 자리, 얼룩, 얼굴 점 / ＊ scenic spot 경치 좋은 곳 / ＊ spotless 흠 없는

   ▪ **상 황**

   Smith : Congratulations! You are both being transferred to the overseas branch.
   (축하해! 너네 둘 다 해외 지사로 옮겨지게 되었어.)

   Yuna : Wow, I got the spot! (우와! 내가 그 자리를 갖게 됐다니!)

   ▪ **응용문제**

   A : I heard you auditioned for the play. (너 연극 오디션 봤다고 들었어.)

   B : Yes, and guess what? _____! (응, 그리고 어떻게 되었을까? 내가 뽑혔어!)

2. **Speak of the devil** 호랑이도 제 말하면 온다.

   ▪ **표현설명**

   중세 "Speak of the Devil and he shall appear."

   ▪ **상황**

   Mike : Did Mr. Brown tell you that? (브라운 사장님한테 들은 거니?)

   Yuna : No, I overheard him. Oh, speak of the devil – here he comes.
   (아니, 사장님께서 얘기하는 걸 들었어. 호랑이도 제 말하면 온다더니, 사장님 오신다.)

   ▪ **응용문제**

   A : Oh, I can't believe Jinny and Tom are going out!
   (아, 지니와 탐이 사귄다니 안 믿겨!)

   B : I know! She's too good for him. (내 말이! 여자가 너무 아까워.)

   A : Oh, careful. _____, they are coming towards us.
   (아, 말조심해야겠다. 호랑이도 제 말하면 온다더니. 둘이 우리 쪽으로 걸어오네.)

04 Pattern Practice

1. Basic

I am going to Ⓥ ~. (내가 ~를 할 예정이다.)

1 나는 그녀를 (데이트하러) 데리고 갈 예정이야.

I am going to _____.

2 나는 파티를 열 예정이야.

I am going to _____.

3 나는 머리할 예정이야.

I am going to _____.

2. One Step Further

What am I going to Ⓥ ~? (내가 ~를 할까?)

1 무엇을 사면 그녀가 기뻐할까?

What am I going to _____?

2 파티 때 어떤 옷을 입을까?

What am I going to _____?

3 근사한 식당에서 무엇을 마실까?

What am I going to _____?

05 TOEIC 실전 문제 풀이

1. **For starters,** you should wear a life vest to enjoy rafting.

   a. Challenger
   b. First of all
   c. Corporate leader
   d. Workers

   HINT for(전치사)와 starters(명사) 결합 → 전치사구 형성

2. This electronic file should be **transferred** to another computer.

   a. moved
   b. delete
   c. proofread
   d. changed

   HINT 품사 고려 후 의미로 결정

3. Be sure to complete an _____ and have it ready with your resume.

   a. apply
   b. applicable
   c. applying
   d. application

   HINT V+a(n)+N 패턴 찾기

06 Auto-Memorization

1. **Working / Tourist Visa** : 워킹 / 관광 비자

   A passport, a working visa

2. **International driver's license** : 국제 운전면허증

3. **overseas branch** : 해외 지사

   You are both being transferred to the overseas branch.

4. **application** : 지원서

   I heard your job application for the US branch has been accepted.

5. **transfer** : 옮기다, 발령되다

6. **for starters** : 우선

   For starters, a passport, a working visa and an international driver's license

07 Wrap Up

1. 연상 퀴즈

1 A : How was the interview? (인터뷰 어땠어?)

B : It was pretty tough, but _____. (조금 어려웠지만 내가 그 자리에 뽑혔어.)

2 A : Jane's new hairdo is awful! (제인의 새로운 머리 스타일 정말 이상해!)

B : Shh... _____, she is right behind you.
(쉿… 호랑이도 제 말 하면 온다더니, 너 바로 뒤에 있어.)

2. Tapping

- International driver's license : 국제 운전면허증
- overseas branch : 해외 지사

3. Pattern

나는 그녀에게 사귀자고 말할 예정이야.

I am going to (ask her out / tell her that I have a crush on her / ask her out for a date).

*사귀다 : see each other, go out

과제 작문 연습

Key phrase를 가지고 두 사람이 대화를 하는 상황을 만들어 보세요.

Key phrase : **Speak of the devil**

 **Culture Tip**

* 미국 무비자 ESTA 신청하기

전자여행허가제인 ESTA는 2년 동안 미국 비자 없이 90일간 미국을 수시로 방문할 수 있는 비자 면제 프로그램이다. ESTA을 신청하려면 반드시 전자 여권이 있어야 한다. 또한 출국 전에 입국 승인 허가를 받아야 한다.

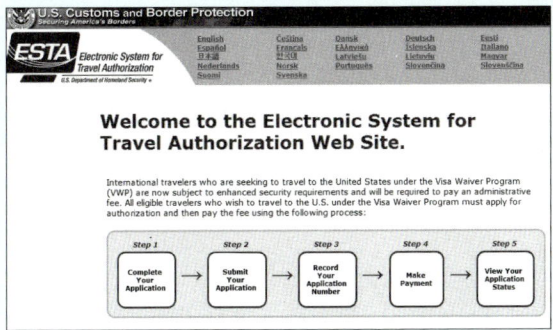

1. https://esta.cbp.dhs.gov/esta/ 홈페이지에 들어간다.
2. 21개의 언어로 볼 수 있지만 응답은 영어로 작성해야 한다.
3. 신청 번호를 기억해둔다.
4. 신청 허가에 대한 답을 약 2주 뒤에 받는다.

 참고 사이트

* **교수님 블로그 사이트**
http://blog.daum.net/tasteofny/42?srchid=BR1http%3A%2F%2Fblog.daum.net%2Ftasteofny%2F42V

* **VISA 내국인 발급 안내**
http://www.immigration.go.kr/HP/IMM/imm_04/imm_0401/imm_040103/imm_401030.jsp

* **VISA LA 발급 안내**
http://www.passportsandvisas.com/localpassport/losangelespassport.asp

Chapter 02

Checking In for the Flight

Topic	Checking In for the Flight
Summary	Mike and Yuna are at the airport, getting ready for their overseas flight. They are checking in their luggage.

주제	여행 가방 수속
줄거리	마이크와 유나는 비행기를 타러 공항에 있다. 그들은 여행 가방을 수속하려고 한다.

Pre-check Quiz ✳

Q. 다음 중 의미 설명이 틀린 것을 고르시오.

   a. baggage allowance – 수하물 허용량

   b. put on – 올려 놓다

   c. check in – 탑승하다

   d. pieces of baggage – 몇 개의 가방

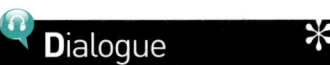

Dialogue ✳

(GC : Ground Crew)

GC   Good afternoon. May I see your passports and tickets please?

Yuna   Sure, here you go.

GC   And how many pieces of baggage will you be checking in today?

Mike   We have four bags to check in.

GC   Okay, I'll just need to weigh those. Could you put them on the belt, please?

Mike   Wait, it seems, these weigh a ton. I think they will be over the baggage allowance.

- -

GC   안녕하세요. 여권과 티켓 좀 보여주시겠어요?

유나   여기 있습니다.

GC   오늘 부칠 짐이 몇 개 있으십니까?

마이크   총 4개 있습니다.

GC   알겠습니다. 무게를 재야겠네요. 여기 벨트 위에 짐을 올려놓아 주세요.

마이크   잠시만요, 이거 진짜 무거운데요. 수하물이 허용량을 초과할 것 같네요.

01 Comprehension Questions

1. Which items did the ground crew ask for?

   a. bag
   b. luggage and ticket
   c. passport and ticket
   d. luggage

   HINT May I see your passports and tickets please?

2. What does Yuna mean by saying "What is my baggage allowance"?

   a. to ask how many bags she can hand-carry on plane
   b. to ask which bag is hers
   c. to ask how much weight of baggage she can check in
   d. to ask if she could get a discount on overweight charge

   HINT What is the maximum weight of baggage?

02 Vocabulary

1. check in : 공항 탑승 수속, 짐을 부치다, 투숙하다

   (=the process of announcing your arrival or the arrival of your baggage)

2. four bags vs. four pieces of baggage : 여행 가방

   bags vs. baggage는 복수로 만들 때 piece를 사용

3. baggage allowance : 수하물 허용량

   (=a term indicating how much baggage is permitted to be carried during your trip)

   allowance ⓝ 규칙적으로 주어지는 돈

4. put on : 올려 놓다 (=to place somewhere)

   Could you put them on the belt?

1. **How many bags will you be checking in today?** 오늘 부칠 짐이 몇 개인가요?

상황

GC : Passports and tickets please. How many bags will you be checking in?
(여권과 티켓 좀 보여주세요. 가방은 몇 개 수송하실 건가요?)

Yuna : Just 1 bag. (1개요.)

응용문제

A : Let's see… These ones should be checked in… No, this one shouldn't. Ugh, but that one should…Or should it? Oh God!
(자, 보자…… 이것들은 부쳐야 되고…… 아냐, 이건 부치면 안 돼. 으악, 하지만 저건 부쳐야 되는데…… 안 부쳐도 되나? 어떡하면 좋아!)

B : Okay, that's it! _____?
(아 좀 그만해요! 그래서 오늘 부칠 짐은 도대체 몇 개예요?)

2. **It seems, these weigh a ton.** 이거 진짜 무거운 거 같은데요.

상황

GC : Okay, I'll just need to weigh those. Could you put them on the belt, please?
(알겠습니다. 무게를 재야겠네요. 여기 벨트 위에 짐을 올려놓아 주세요.)

Mike : It seems, these weigh a ton. (잠시만요, 이거 진짜 무거운데요.)

응용문제

A : Hey sweetie, I feel so dizzy. Can you give me a piggy-back? Please……
(자기야, 나 너무 어지러워. 업어주면 안 돼? 제발…)

B : Hmm, to be frank, _____. Was it a lie that you've lost some weight? (솔직히 말하자면, 너 진짜 무거워. 살 빠졌다는 거 거짓말이었니?)

04 **P**attern Practice

1. Basic

Put something on ~ / Put on ~ (명령문 : 무엇을 ~에 올려놔.)

1 테이블에 너의 핸드폰을 올려놓아라.

_____.

2 선글라스를 껴라.

Put on _____.

3 귀걸이를 해라.

Put on _____.

2. One Step Further

Why don't you ~? (완고한 요청 : ~하는 것은 어때?)

1 너의 핸드폰을 테이블에 올려두지 않을래?

Why don't you _____?

2 선글라스를 끼는 게 어때? 바깥이 너무 밝다.

Why don't you _____? It's way too bright outside.

3 모자 쓰는 게 어때? 오늘 머리 안 감은 거 다 알고 있어.

Why don't you _____? I know you didn't shampoo today.

1. This baggage seems like it <u>weighs a ton</u>.

   a. is very heavy   b. is a ton weight

   c. is too complex   d. is not allowed to be checked in

2. The <u>baggage allowance</u> is less than 20 kilos per person.

   a. hand-carry baggage   b. overweight bags

   c. travel bags   d. approved baggage weight

3. Please <u>put your tickets on</u> the check-in counter.

   a. place your tickets on   b. puts your ticket

   c. puts your jacket on   d. weigh your tickets on

06 Auto-Memorization

1. check in : 탑승 수속

   We have four bags to check in.

2. four pieces of baggage : 여행 가방 4개

   You have checked in four pieces of baggage.

3. baggage allowance : 수하물 허용량

   I think they will be over the baggage allowance.

4. put on : 올려 놓다

   Put them on the belt.

1. 연상 퀴즈

   1 A : Where did you go just now?
   (방금 어디 갔다 왔어?)

   B : I went to the counter to _____.
   (잠시 탑승 수속하러 카운터에 갔었어.)

   2 A : Can you move this washing machine by yourself?
   (혼자서 이 세탁기를 옮길 수 있나요?)

   B : I'm not sure. It feels like this machine _____.
   (잘 모르겠어요. 이 세탁기 굉장히 무거워 보이네요.)

2. Tapping

   • check in : 탑승 수속

   • baggage allowance : 수하물 허용량

   • put on : 올려 놓다

3. Pattern

   모자를 써라.

   Put on (your hat).

📺 과제 작문 연습

   Key phrase를 가지고 두 사람이 대화를 하는 상황을 만들어 보세요.

   Key phrase : **It feels like it weighs a ton.**

＊US Immigration 입국심사

9.11 테러 이후로 미국은 입국 심사가 극도로 강화되었고 입국 심사 과정에 지문을 찍고 얼굴 사진을 찍게 되어있다.

① 왼쪽 네 손가락의 지문을 찍는다.

② 오른쪽 네 손가락의 지문을 찍는다.

③ 마지막으로 엄지 손가락 두 개의 지문을 찍는다.

④ 지문이 끝난 후 "Please look at the camera."라는 요청을 받는다. 이때 웹 캠을 바라보고 얼굴 사진을 찍게 된다.

 참고 사이트

＊Baggage Allowance—수하물 허용량에 대한 정보

http://www.aa.com/i18n/travelInformation/baggage/baggageAllowance.jsp

Chapter 03

Immigration
Interview

Topic	Immigration Interview
Summary	Yuna has arrived at the Los Angeles International airport. Before she leaves, she's having a short interview with the immigration agent.

주제	출입국 관리소 인터뷰
줄거리	유나는 LA 국제 공항에 도착했다. 공항을 떠나기 전에 출입국 관리소 직원과 간단한 인터뷰를 하고 있다.

Pre-check Quiz ✳

Q. 다음 중 의미 설명이 틀린 것을 고르시오.

a. What brings you to ~? – (~에는) 무슨 일로 오셨나요?

b. purpose – 목적

c. top notch – 최고의

d. stay – 머물다

e. for the time being – 여태껏

🎧 Dialogue ✳

(IA : Immigration Agent)

IA   May I see your passport please? What is the purpose of your visit? I mean, what brings you to America?

Yuna   Well, I am here to take a language program at UCLA. Thanks to my company. (Shrug)

IA   Wow. That's a top notch school. Then, where are you going to stay?

Yuna   Well, for the time being, I'll be at the youth hostel.

IA   Okay, good luck with your program. Enjoy the California sunshine.

Yuna   Thank you.

- -

IA   잠시 여권 좀 볼 수 있겠습니까? 방문 목적이 무엇이시죠? 제 말은, 무슨 일로 미국을 방문하게 되었습니까?

유나   UCLA에서 어학 연수 프로그램을 이수하기로 했어요. 회사가 보내주는 거예요. (어깨를 으쓱거리며)

IA   와, 명문 대학교에 가시네요. 그러면 어디서 묵을 예정인가요?

유나   음, 일단은 유스호스텔에서 머물려고 합니다.

IA   알겠습니다. 공부 잘 하시길 빌어요. 캘리포니아의 햇살을 만끽하세요.

유나   감사합니다.

01 Comprehension Questions

1. Where does Yuna say she will be staying?

   a. for the time being   b. her friend

   c. at a youth hostel   d. at a nice hotel

   HINT Well, for the time being, I'll be staying at a youth hostel.

2. Why is Yuna coming to America?

   a. She wants to tour California's universities.

   b. She wants to study California.

   c. She loves working hard.

   d. She plans to study at the Univ. of California.

   HINT Well, I am here to take a language program at UCLA.

02 Vocabulary

1. **What brings you to ~?** : (~에는) 무슨 일로 오셨나요?

   (=What is your reason for being here?)

2. **purpose** : 목적

   My purpose in writing this letter to you is to ask for a raise.

3. **top notch** : 최고의 (=the best or one of the best; well-known)

   It's one of the top notch restaurants in the business.

4. **stay** : 머물다 (=lodge; can also be used in lieu of 'sleep')

   So if all the hotels are full, where do you plan to stay tonight?

5. **for the time being** : 당분간 (time being=right now; at the moment, for now)

   For the time being, I do not have a place to live.

1. **What's the purpose of your visit?** 방문 목적이 뭔가요?

   표현설명

   =What is the reason of your being here?

   상황

   IA : May I see your passport, please? What is the purpose of your visit? I mean, what brings you to America?

   (잠시 여권 좀 볼 수 있겠습니까? 방문 목적이 무엇이시죠? 제 말은, 어쩐 일로 미국을 방문하게 되었습니까?)

   응용문제 1

   JY : Hi, Mr. Johnson. _____? (안녕하세요, 존슨씨. 한국에 무슨 일로 오셨나요?)

   Mr. J : I am here on business. (출장차 방문하였습니다.)

   응용문제 2

   JY : Hi, Mr. Johnson. _____? (안녕하세요, 존슨씨. 한국에 무슨 일로 오셨나요?)

   Mr. J : I am here on vacation (for leisure/to visit my relatives/to study).

   (여기에 휴가 왔어요/놀러 왔어요/친척을 방문하러 왔어요/공부하러 왔어요)

2. **Wow. That's a top notch school.** 우와. 거기는 최고의 학교잖아.

   표현설명

   =That school is one of the best in the country.

   상황

   Yuna : Well, I am here to take a language program at UCLA. Thanks to my company.

   (UCLA로 어학 연수 프로그램을 받기로 했어요. 회사가 보내주는 거예요.)

   IA : Wow. That's a top notch school. (와, 명문 대학교에 가시네요.)

Anne : So which university did you get into? (너 어느 대학 들어갔니?)

Min Ju : Seoul National University. It's the _____ school in Korea.
(서울대학교. 한국 최고의 학교지.)

3. **Where [are you going to stay/will you be staying]?** 어디서 머무를 예정이니?

표현설명

=Where will you sleep tonight? Where are you lodging during your vacation?

상황

IA : Then, where are you going to stay? (그러면 어디서 묵을 예정이십니까?)

Yuna : Well, for the time being, I'll be at the youth hostel.
(음, 일단은 유스호스텔에서 머물려고 합니다.)

응용문제

Chul : _____ in Washington? (워싱턴 어디서 머무를 거니?)

Eun Jung : At my grandparents'. (할아버지 댁에서.)

4. **Enjoy the California sunshine.** 캘리포니아의 햇빛을 만끽해.

표현설명

Idiom meaning "enjoy your visit"; If the person were visiting Alaska it would be appropriate to say, "Enjoy the cold!"

상황

IA : Okay, good luck with your program. Enjoy the California sunshine.
(알겠습니다. 공부 잘 하시길 빌어요. 캘리포니아의 햇살을 만끽하세요.)

Yuna : Thank you. (감사합니다.)

Ji Min : To Sacramento, please. I want to get a tan.

(세크리멘토 가주세요. 선탠하고 싶거든요.)

Taxi driver : You'll get sick and tired of the sun. Just kidding. _____!

(너 햇빛이 지긋지긋해질 거야. 농담이고 캘리포니아 햇빛을 만끽하렴.)

04 Pattern Practice

1. Basic

May I see/take a look at ~? (요청 : ~를 잠시 볼 수 있겠습니까?)

1 선생님, 스마트 폰을 좀 볼 수 있을까요?

May I see _____?

2 (정중) 네 시험 대비 노트 좀 볼 수 있을까?

May I see _____?

3 (경찰, 직원이) 잠시 신분증 좀 확인할 수 있을까요?

May I see _____?

2. One Step Further

You may see ~. (허락 : ~을 보아도 돼.)

1 스마트 폰 봐도 되지만 조심해.

You may see _____.

2 시험 대비 노트를 봐도 되긴 하지만, 돌려보지 마.

You may see _____.

3 신분증 보셔도 돼요. 전 23살입니다.

You may see _____. _____.

05 TOEIC 실전 문제 풀이

1. The main _____ of this presentation is to introduce our company.

   a. resolve   b. intend

   c. strength   d. purpose

   HINT 형용사(main) + 명사(purpose) 유형

2. Samsung Electronics is a _____ corporation with its history and size.

   a. history   b. top notch

   c. challenging   d. indifference

   HINT is 다음에 a(관사) + 형용사 + 명사(corporation)의 구조가 와야 한다.

3. Let's not see each other for _____.

   a. the time being   b. a good

   c. on purpose   d. sale

   HINT '당분간'이라는 표현 찾기

06 Auto-Memorization

1. What brings you to A? : A에는 무슨 일로 오셨나요?

   What brings you to America?

2. purpose : 목적

   What is the purpose of your visit?

3. top notch : 최고의, 명문의

   That's a top notch school.

4. stay : 머물다

   Where are you going to stay?

5. for the time being : 당분간

   For the time being I'll be at the youth hostel.

1. 연상 퀴즈

1 A : Surprise! Here I am!
  (놀랐지! 나 왔어!)

  B : Oh my god, _____ here?
  (어머나, 여기 어쩐 일이니?)

2 A : I don't have much money to stay at a hotel. What should I do?
  (호텔에서 묵을만한 돈이 없는데 어떡하지?)

  B : Why don't you stay in the _____?
  (유스호스텔에서 숙박하는 건 어때?)

2. Tapping

- top notch : 최고의, 명문의
- purpose : 목적
- for the time being : 당분간은

3. Pattern

저기에 있는 셔츠 봐도 됩니까?

May I see (the shirt over there)?

🖥 과제 작문 연습

Key phrase를 가지고 두 사람이 대화를 하는 상황을 만들어 보세요.

Key phrase : **What is the purpose of your visit?**

 Culture Tip

＊Immigration - 입국 심사

When you are visiting America, depending on which airport you land, the immigration officer can ask you different questions. For example, in LA, Chicago, San Francisco, New York and other big cities where many Koreans visit, the questions asked would be simple. However, in places where Koreans rarely visit such as Portland, the officer may ask you questions that are hard to answer, and if you are unlucky you may be kicked out. So you should smile and greet the officer 'Hi' in a friendly manner and then tell the purpose of visit truthfully.

미국을 방문할 때는 어떤 공항을 통해서 들어가느냐 따라 이민관의 질문 정도가 달라진다. 예를 들어, 한국인이 많이 들락거리는 LA나 Chicago, San Francisco, New York 등의 도시는 질문이 아주 간단하지만 한국 사람이 많이 입국하지 않는 Portland 등은 질문도 까다롭고 운이 아주 나쁘면 그냥 쫓겨날 수도 있다. 우선 이민관 앞에 서면 밝게 웃으며 'Hi' 라고 인사를 하는 것이 좋다. 그리고 사실대로 입국 목적을 말하면 된다.

 참고 사이트

＊Los Angeles 공항 정보
http://www.lawa.org/welcomelax.aspx

Chapter 04

Asking for
Directions

Topic	Asking for Directions
Summary	Mike is asking for directions at the gas station.

주제	길 물어보기
줄거리	마이크가 주유소에서 길을 묻는다.

Q. 다음 중 의미 설명이 틀린 것을 고르시오.

a. gas station – 주유소

b. regular – 보통

c. diesel – 경유·중유 등 디젤 연료

d. directions – 지도

Dialogue ✱

Mike	Geez, I need to ask someone for directions. Oh, there's a gas station.
W	Afternoon. You want regular or diesel?
Mike	Actually, umm... We're not here to fill up the gas. How do I get to 'Universal Studios'?
W	Go straight; hang a left at the first corner and you'll see a pizza place.
Mike	OK, what's next?
W	Just follow the signs with the big globe that say 'Universal'. You can't miss it.

마이크	우리 누구한테 길을 물어봐야 할 거 같아. 아, 저기 주유소 있다.
W	안녕하세요. 보통 휘발유를 넣을까요, 경유를 넣을까요?
마이크	사실, 음… 저희는 기름을 넣으려고 온 게 아니에요. 유니버셜 스튜디오에 어떻게 가나요?
W	쭉 직진하시다가 첫 코너에서 왼쪽으로 돌면 피자집이 보일 거예요.
마이크	피자집에서 어떻게 가죠?
W	'유니버셜'이라고 써있는 간판을 따라가시면 돼요. 놓칠 수 없을 거예요.

01 Comprehension Questions

1. **Where is the Mike's final destination?**

   a. The gas station
   b. The pizza restaurant
   c. Universal Studios
   d. The first corner

   HINT How do I get to Universal Studios?

2. **Why does Mike stop at the gas station?**

   a. He wants to fill up the gas.
   b. He wants to eat some pizza.
   c. He has arrived at Universal Studios.
   d. He is lost.

   HINT We're not here to fill up the gas. How do I get to 'Universal Studios'?

02 Vocabulary

1. **gas station** : 주유소 (=place people go to fill up the gas in their cars)
   We always stop at the gas station on Main Street because they have the best prices.

2. **regular or diesel** : 일반 휘발유 또는 경유 (=two different types of gasoline)
   The attendant asked if we wanted regular or diesel, but he should know that we need diesel because I drive an old BMW.

3. **fill up the gas** : 기름을 (가득) 넣다
   (=add fuel to the tank of a vehicle until it is filled to maximum capacity)
   This car gets really good mileage so we only have to fill up the gas a few times a month.

4. **go straight** : 직진으로 가다 (=go forward without turning)
   To get to the post office just go straight for three blocks and it's on the left.

5. **hang a left/right** : 왼쪽/오른쪽으로 돌다 (=turn/make a left)
   If you hang a right at the next corner you'll see the movie theater in front of you.

Expressions

1. **I need to ask someone for directions.** 누구에게 길을 물어봐야 할 거 같다.

표현설명

= Since we cannot find the destination ourselves, it is necessary that we inquire of somebody how to locate the place.

상황

Mike : Geez, I need to ask someone for directions. Oh, there's a gas station.
(우리 누구한테 길을 물어봐야 할 거 같아. 아 저기 주유소 있다.)

응용문제

A : We have been driving around here for three hours!
(우리 지금 3시간째 여기서 운전하고 있어!)

B : What should we do? (어떻게 해야 되지?)

A : _____. (누구에게 길을 물어봐야 할 것 같아.)

2. **How do I get to ~?** ~에 어떻게 가나요?

표현설명

= Which way should I go in order to reach ~ ?

상황

Mike : Actually, umm... We're not here to fill up the gas. How do I get to 'Universal Studios'? (사실, 음… 저희는 기름 넣으려 온 게 아니에요. 유니버셜 스튜디오에 어떻게 가나요?)

W   : Go straight; hang a left at the first corner and you'll see a pizza place.
(쭉 직진하시다가 코너에서 왼쪽으로 돌면 피자집이 보일 거예요.)

A : Wow. We are literally lost. Let's ask the woman over there how to get to the post office. (우리 지금 그야말로 길을 잃었어. 저기 있는 여자한테 우체국에 어떻게 가는지 물어 보자.)

B : I am too shy. You ask. (나는 쑥스러워서 못해. 네가 물어봐.)

A : Excuse me. _____? (실례합니다. 우체국에 어떻게 가나요?)

3. You can't miss it. 놓칠 수 없을 거예요.

= It is so easy to find that you will definitely see it, guaranteed.

W : Just follow the signs with the big globe that say 'Universal'. You can't miss it.
('유니버셜'이라고 써 있는 간판을 따라가시면 돼요. 놓칠 수 없을 거예요.)

A : Go straight and you'll see a huge stadium. (쭉 직진하면 큰 경기장이 보일 거예요.)

B : What's the name of the street? (도로 이름이 뭐죠?)

A : I'm not sure, but _____. It's the biggest building in the city!
(잘은 모르지만 놓칠 수 없을 거예요. 도시에서 가장 큰 빌딩이거든요!)

A : If you want to get to the fire station, just hang a left at the corner.
(소방서에 가려면 코너에서 왼쪽으로 도세요.)

B : But how will I know when I've reached it? (하지만 제가 거기 도착했다는 걸 어떻게 알아요?)

A : It's the big red building with all the flashing lights. _____.
(반짝이는 불빛들이 가득한 큰 빨간 빌딩이에요. 놓칠 수 없을 거예요.)

1. Basic

> **How do I get to ~?** (~에 어떻게 가나요?)

1 디즈니랜드에 어떻게 가나요?

How do I get to _____?

2 한인 타운에 어떻게 가나요?

How do I get to _____?

3 산타 모니카 해변에 어떻게 가나요?

How do I get to _____?

4 할리우드에 어떻게 가나요?

How do I get to _____?

2. One Step Further

> **You can get to ~.** (~에 가실 수 있습니다.)

1 디즈니랜드에 버스로 가실 수 있습니다.

You can get to _____.

2 한인 타운에 지하철 타고 가실 수 있습니다.

You can get to _____.

3 산타 모니카 해변에 걸어서 가실 수 있습니다.

You can get to _____.

4 자가용으로 할리우드에 가실 수 있습니다.

You can get to _____.

1. Please fill _____ this glass with orange juice.

   a. out   b. up

   c. with   d. over

   HINT Eat it up. : 남기지 말고 다 먹어라.

2. _____ left at this block, and you'll see the office building.

   a. Skip   b. Traverse

   c. Hang a   d. Pound

   HINT Hang a left.＝Turn left.

3. Let's _____ him. He knows the way.

   a. follow   b. follow to

   c. follow with   d. follow for

   HINT 전치사가 필요 없는 타동사

06 Auto-**M**emorization

1. gas station : 주유소

   Oh, there's a gas station.

2. regular or diesel : 일반 휘발유 또는 경유

   You want regular or diesel?

3. fill up the gas : 기름을 (가득) 넣다

   We're not here to fill up the gas.

4. go straight : 직진으로 가다

   Go straight and you'll see a pizza place.

5. hang a left/right＝turn/make a left : 왼쪽/오른쪽으로 돌다

   Hang a left at the first corner.

1. 연상 퀴즈

1 A : Excuse me, which is the fastest highway to Springfield?
(실례합니다. 스프링필드로 가는 제일 빠른 고속도로는 어느 쪽이죠?)

B : Go straight, _____ and turn left once more in 5 minutes.
(직진하다가 왼쪽으로 한 번 꺾고 5분 뒤에 또 한 번 왼쪽으로 꺾으세요.)

2 A : What a nice car! Which gasoline does it use, _____?
(정말 좋은 차구나. 휘발유와 경유 중 어떤 기름을 쓰니?)

B : Actually, it uses solar energy. It's an environment friendly car.
(사실, 이 차는 태양열로 가동이 되는 환경친화적인 자동차야.)

2. Tapping

- regular or diesel : 일반 휘발유 또는 경유
- go straight : 직진하다
- gas station : 주유소

3. Pattern

유니버셜 스튜디오에 택시 타고 가실 수 있습니다.

You can get to (Universal Studio by taxi).

📺 과제 작문 연습

Key phrase를 가지고 두 사람이 대화를 하는 상황을 만들어 보세요.

Key phrase : **You can't miss it.**

 ## Culture Tip

∗ Go to AAA if you are lost in LA (LA에서 길을 잃었을 때 AAA 찾아가기)

AAA is a road service car club that is most frequently used by Americans. They provide hotel reservation, rental cars, tough, emergency fuel supplement, jump start and other services. If you are lost on the road, find an AAA office and you can receive services such as point-to-point route, advices on restaurants and tourist attractions where they will kindly mark on the map for you. There are almost 100 branches in LA alone.

AAA는 미국 사람들이 가장 많이 사용하는 roadside service 자동차 클럽이다. AAA는 호텔 예약, 렌터카, 견인, 비상시 휘발유 보충, 점프 스타트 등의 서비스를 제공한다. 특히 가장 많이 사용되는 서비스로, 길을 잃었을 때 AAA office로 가면 지도 위에 표시하면서 point to point 운전 경로, 레스토랑, 관광포인트 등에 대한 조언을 해준다. LA에만도 100개 정도의 지사가 있다.

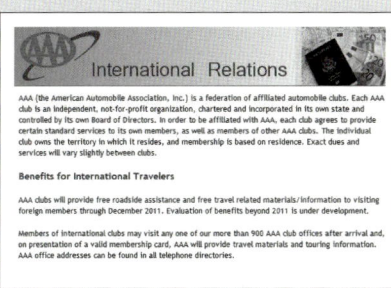

 참고 사이트

∗ AAA 홈페이지
http://www.aaa.com/scripts/WebObjects.dll/ZipCode.woa/wa/route?rclub=065&stop=yes&rur
http://www.ouraaa.com/aaainfo/offices/index.html

Chapter 05

Shopping at the
Flea **M**arket

Topic	Shopping at the Flea Market
Summary	Yuna is at the flea market and she is bargaining with the owner for a couch she likes.

주제	벼룩시장에서 쇼핑하기
줄거리	유나는 벼룩 시장에서 마음에 드는 소파의 가격을 주인과 흥정하고 있다.

Q. 다음 중 의미 설명이 틀린 것을 고르시오.

a. mint condition − 상태가 양호하다

b. asking price − 마지막 제안

c. best offer − 적정가

d. delivery service − 배달 서비스

Dialogue ✳

Yuna	Wow, that's a nice La-Z-Boy you have there!
M	Thanks. It's only two years old and it's still in mint condition.
Yuna	So what's your asking price?
M	$100 or your best offer.
Yuna	I'll give you 70 bucks, what do you say?
M	You trying to bleed me dry here? 85 dollars, but no delivery service included. That's my final offer.
Yuna	Okay, it's a deal. It's a steal anyway.

유나	우와. 이 La-Z-Boy 의자 정말 좋네요.
M	감사합니다. 2년밖에 안 썼기 때문에 상태가 아직 양호합니다.
유나	그럼 얼마에 파실 건가요?
M	$100 생각하고 있는데 생각하시는 적정가가 있으신가요?
유나	70불 드리겠습니다. 어떤가요?
M	제 돈을 다 쥐어짜 내려고 하시나요? 배달 서비스 없이 85불에 드리겠습니다. 그게 마지막 제안이에요.
유나	네, 받아드리겠습니다. 어차피 거저 가격인데요.

1. How long has the seller used La-Z-Boy?

   a. two years

   b. two months

   c. two weeks

   d. two decades

   > HINT It's only two years old and it's still in mint condition.

2. How much is the man's final offer?

   a. 100 dollars

   b. 8 bucks

   c. 85 bucks

   d. 75 dollars

   > HINT 85 dollars, but no delivery service included. That's my final offer.

02 Vocabulary

1. best offer : 적정가, 판매자의 제일 낮은 가격대

   So, what is your best offer?

2. delivery service : 배달 서비스

   85 dollars, but no delivery service included.

3. final offer : 마지막 제안 (=last offer)

   (판매자와 구매자가 각자의 best offer을 놓고 흥정한 후) That's my final offer.

4. deal : 거래가 성사되다, 제안을 받아들이다

   I don't want to argue any more. Let's make a deal, and go home.

5. It is a steal. : 값이 매우 싸다 (=the price is extremely low.)

   It's a steal anyway.

03 Expressions

1. mint condition 양호한 상태

표현설명

=perfect condition; just like new

상황

Yuna : Wow, that's a nice La-Z-Boy you have there! (우와. 이 La-Z-Boy 의자 정말 좋네요.)

M : Thanks. It's only two years old and it's still in mint condition.
(감사합니다. 2년 밖에 안 썼기 때문에 상태가 아직 양호합니다.)

응용문제 1

A : Here is my old collection of comic books. (자, 여기에 내 오래된 만화 컬렉션이 있어.)

B : Wow! They're almost new. You kept them in _____.
(우와! 정말 새 것 같아. 좋은 상태로 보존했구나.)

응용문제 2

A : How can you expect me to pay that much for a used baseball glove?
(어떻게 나한테 사용한 글러브를 그만큼의 돈을 주고 사게 해?)

B : Come on, I hardly used it at all. It's in _____.
(야, 나 거의 안 썼어. 상태가 양호해.)

2. What's your asking price? 얼마에 파실 건가요?

표현설명

=How much are you selling it for?

상황

Yuna : So what's your asking price? (그럼 얼마에 파실 건가요?)

M : $100 or your best offer. ($100 생각하고 있는데 생각하시는 적정가가 있으신가요?)

A : This bike is about $450 if you buy it online.
(온라인에서 이 자전거를 $450에 살 수 있습니다.)

B : Hmmm okay. So, _____?
(음, 그렇군요. 그렇다면 얼마에 팔 생각인가요?)

A : I've seen this model on sale all over town. _____?
(전 시내에서 이 모델을 할인하고 있어요. 저한테 얼마에 팔 건가요?)

B : $18.95 and you won't find it any cheaper than that.
($18.95에 드릴게요. 이 가격보다 싼 곳은 찾을 수 없을 거예요.)

3. **bleed somebody dry** (~의) 돈을 다 쥐어짜 내다

= take all of somebody's money; extort somebody

Yuna : I'll give you 70 bucks, what do you say? (70불 드리겠습니다. 어떤가요?)

M   : You trying to bleed me dry here? (제 돈을 다 쥐어짜 내려고 하시나요?)

A : Did you hear about the new tax hike? (세금 인상한다는 소식 들었어?)

B : What? The government raised the tax again? (뭐? 정부가 또 세금 인상을 했어?)

A : Yes, they are going to _____. (응, 우리 돈을 다 뜯어먹을 작정인가 봐.)

A : I can't believe how much you spend on your child's education.
(네가 자녀 교육에 돈을 이만큼 썼다는 사실이 난 믿기지 않아.)

B : Yeah, it's kind of _____, but I think it's all worth it.
(그래, 정말 돈이 많이 들어갔지만, 그만큼 가치가 있다고 생각해.)

4. No delivery service 배달 서비스는 없다

= The customer will have to arrange their own means of delivery.

M : 85 dollars, but no delivery service included. That's my final offer.
(배달 서비스 없이 85불에 드리겠습니다. 그게 마지막 제안이에요.)

Yuna : Okay, it's a deal. It's a steal anyway. (네, 받아드리겠습니다. 어차피 거저 가격인데요.)

A : Do you know a good delivery company? (좋은 배달 회사 알아?)

B : No, why? (아니, 왜?)

A : I bought a fridge but there is _____ included.
(내가 냉장고를 샀는데 배달 서비스는 포함되어 있지 않거든.)

A : I'd like a large pizza with extra cheese. I'm at 351 West Main Street.
(치즈 추가한 라지 피자 하나 주세요. 여기 위치는 351 West Main Street입니다.)

B : Sorry, there's _____ here at Little Gino's Pizza.
(죄송합니다. 여기 Little Gino's Pizza는 배달이 안 됩니다.)

04 **P**attern Practice

1. Basic

I am trying to ~. (열심히 ~을 하려고 노력하는 중이다.)

1 나 살 빼려는 중이야.

I am trying to _____.

2 나는 그녀에게 데이트 신청하려고 해.

I am trying to _____.

3 나는 전부 A학점을 받으려고 노력 중이야.

I am trying to _____.

2. One Step Further

Are you trying to ~? (넌 ~하려고 하니?)

1 너 그녀의 마음을 사려고 하니?

Are you trying to _____?

2 너 그녀의 마음을 아프게 하려고 하니?

Are you trying to _____?

3 너 점수 잘 받으려고 하니?

Are you trying to _____?

1. If your _____ offer is $5, I won't buy this pencil case.

    a. good   b. finalize

    c. final   d. reasonably

    HINT 소유격(your)+명사 구조로 빈칸에는 명사가 와야 한다.

2. Mr. Brown will _____ a speech at a conference.

    a. give birth   b. send

    c. present   d. transport

    HINT delivery가 가진 여러 의미(출산, 배달, 연설) 중 맥락에 맞는 의미를 파악해야 한다.

3. I'll buy this cushion _____ it's a steal.

    a. since   b. because of

    c. however   d. therefore

    HINT It's a steal. = It's very cheap. = It's a good deal. = It's a real bargain.

06 Auto-Memorization

1. best offer : 적정가

    $100 or your best offer

2. delivery service : 배달 서비스

    85 dollars, but no delivery service included.

3. final offer : 마지막 제안

    That's my final offer.

4. deal : 거래가 성사되다

    Okay, deal.

5. It is a steal. : 값이 매우 싸다

    It's a steal anyway.

07 Wrap Up

1. 연상 퀴즈

1 A : Hello, I'd like to order two Big Mac and extra French fries. The address is...
(안녕하세요. 빅맥 세트 두 개랑 감자튀김 하나 부탁 드립니다. 여기는…)

B : Sorry, ma'am. We don't do _____.
(손님, 죄송하지만 저희는 배달을 하지 않습니다.)

2 A : How about this? I'll rent your room for the summer vacation and pay you
$300 a month. (이건 어때? 내가 여름방학 동안 네 방을 빌리고 매달 $300씩 주는 거야.)

B : _____. Which day will you move in? (제안을 받아드리겠어. 며칠에 이사올 예정이니?)

2. Tapping

- deal : 거래가 성사되다
- It's a steal. : 값이 매우 싸다
- best offer : 적정가

3. Pattern

너 나에게 거짓말 하려는 거니?

Are you trying to (lie to me)?

📺 과제 작문 연습

Key phrase를 가지고 두 사람이 대화를 하는 상황을 만들어 보세요.

Key phrase : **What's your asking price?**

 Culture Tip

Rose Bowl Flea Market is LA's largest and most popular antique flea market. The admission price varies depending on the time. It is reasonable to pay 10~20 dollars for admission. The flea market takes place at PASADENA Rose Bowl Stadium every second Sunday of the month. It opens at 6 in the morning and lasts only until 3 p.m. Prices are negotiable but only cash is accepted. Goods that vary in prices as well as antiques are sold.

LA의 가장 큰 벼룩 시장이자 미국에서 가장 유명한 엔티크 시장인 Rose Bowl Flea Market은 입장료가 시간에 따라 다르다. 약 10~20불 정도의 입장료를 내고 들어가는 게 적당하다. 매달 두 번째 일요일에 미식축구 게임이 열리기로 유명한 PASADENA Rose Bowl Stadium에서 열리는 데, 아침 6시에 열며 낮 3시면 장터가 끝난다. 현금 거래만 가능하고 한국처럼 흥정이 된다는 장점을 가지고 있다. 가격이 천차만별인 제품들은 물론이고 골동품도 판매된다.

 참고 사이트

* One of the hippest flea markets in town is the Melrose Trading Post
http://www.melrosetradingpost.org/

* Every second Sunday of the month, Rose Bowl Stadium hosts a huge flea market.
http://www.rosebowlstadium.com/
http://www.rgcshows.com/RoseBowlFleaMarket/tabid/52/Default.aspx

Chapter 06

Go
Sightseeing

Topic   Go Sightseeing

Summary Yuna and Mike are deciding if they should buy the admission tickets to Universal Studio.

주제   관광하기

줄거리 유나와 마이크는 유니버설 스튜디오에서 입장권을 사야 할지를 결정하고 있다.

Pre-check Quiz ✳

Q. 다음 중 의미 설명이 틀린 것을 고르시오.

a. pricey – 상을 받는

b. admission – 입장료

c. go get the ticket – 티켓을 사러 가다

d. worth it – 가치가 있다

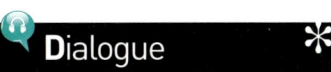 Dialogue ✳

Yuna   Yay! Here we are at last! Let's go sightseeing at 'Universal Studios'! Let's go in.

Mike   You are aware that the admission tickets are kind of pricey, right?

Yuna   Really? How much is admission?

Mike   It's $129 per person.

Yuna   I'm sure it's worth it.

Mike   Okay, you go get the tickets. I need to sit down for awhile. My feet are killing me.

- -

유나   야호! 드디어 왔구나! '유니버셜 스튜디오' 구경하자! 들어가자!

마이크   너 여기 입장료가 매우 비싼 건 알고 있지?

유나   정말? 입장료가 얼만데?

마이크   한 사람당 129달러야.

유나   충분히 그만한 가치가 있을 거야.

마이크   알았어, 그럼 네가 티켓 사와. 난 저기 잠시 앉아 있을게. 다리 아파 죽겠다.

01 Comprehension Questions

1. How much should Mike and Yuna pay for admission?

   a. $258 each   b. $129 each

   c. $258 in total   d. $129 in total

   HINT How much is admission? It's $129 per person.

2. Mike needs to sit down because his shoes are _____ him.

   a. hurt   b. suffer

   c. hurting   d. pain

   HINT I need to sit down for awhile. My feet are killing me.

02 Vocabulary

1. be aware of : 알고 있다 (= know)

   Are you aware of the fact that pollution is destroying the earth?

2. pricey : 비싸다 (= costly; expensive; dear(B.E.))

   This wine is a bit pricey, but my friend Ken absolutely adores it.

3. admission (fee) : 입장료 (= the price of entrance)

   The admission fee for adults is twice that of the students' price.

4. go get the ticket : 티켓 사러 가다 (= go buy the ticket)

   You go get the tickets, and I'll go get the popcorn.

5. worth it : 가치가 있는

   (= the value of the experience is equal to or greater than the price)

   Tickets to Hawaii are pretty expensive, but the experience is totally worth it.

1. **The admission ticket is very pricey.** 입장권 가격이 매우 비싸다.

  상황

  Yuna : Let's go in. (들어가자!)

  Mike : You are aware that the admission tickets are kind of pricey, right?
  (너 여기 입장료가 매우 비싼 건 알고 있지?)

  응용문제

  A : Wait here. I'll go get the tickets. (여기서 잠깐 기다려. 표 사올게.)

  B : But I've heard the _____.
  (근데 여기 입장권이 매우 비싸다고 들었어.)

2. **How much is admission?** 입장료가 얼마입니까?

  상황

  Yuna : How much is admission? (입장료가 얼만데?)

  Mike : It's $129 per person. (한 사람당 129달러야.)

  응용문제

  A : Welcome to the museum. (박물관에 오신 것을 환영합니다.)

  B : _____? (입장료가 얼마입니까?)

  A : Five dollars for adults and $2.50 for children under 12.
  (어른들은 $5이며, 12살 아래인 아동들은 $2.50입니다.)

3. **My feet are killing me.** 다리 아파 죽겠다.

  상황

  Mike : Okay, you go get the tickets. I need to sit down for awhile. My feet are killing me.
  (알았어, 그럼 네가 티켓 사와. 난 저기 잠시 앉아 있을게. 다리 아파 죽겠다.)

A : Oh, man _____. (아, 정말 다리 아파 죽겠다.)

B : Hurry up! Let's go. (서둘러! 어서 가자.)

04 Pattern Practice

1. Basic

~ is killing me. (~때문에 골치가 아파.)

1 숙제 때문에 골치가 아파.

_____

2 하이힐 때문에 죽겠어.

_____

3 이 프로젝트 발표 때문에 죽겠어.

_____

2. One Step Further

~ is a killer ~. (~는 정말 죽여줘.)

1 이 강의 죽여줘.

_____

2 가수 비는 몸에 식스펙이 있어. 정말 죽여줘.

_____

3 내가 좋아하는 여자 아이는 죽이는 목소리를 가지고 있어.

_____

05 TOEIC 실전 문제 풀이

1. This off-season jacket was fairly expensive _____ the new arrival was reasonable.

   a. because of   b. due to

   c. whereas   d. after all

   HINT 주어＋동사 _____ 주어＋동사 사이에는 접속사가 들어가야 한다.

2. _____ you enjoy studying, there will be no regret.

   a. As long as   b. Besides

   c. In case of   d. Along with

   HINT 뒤에 '주어＋동사'가 올 수 있는 접속사 고르기

3. You should _____ of the fact that foxes are aggressive here.

   a. know   b. be fond

   c. be aware   d. are aware

   HINT 〈should＋be＋동사원형〉 구문에 맞는 답 고르기

06 Auto-Memorization

1. be aware of : ～을 알고 있다

   You are aware that the admission tickets are kind of pricey, right?

2. pricey : 비싸다

3. admission (fee) : 입장료

   How much is admission?

4. go get the ticket : 가서 티켓을 사다

   Okay, you go get the tickets.

5. worth it : 그만한 가치가 있는

   I'm sure it's worth it.

Wrap Up

1. 연상 퀴즈

   1 A : You are aware that the admission tickets are kind of pricey, right?
      (입장료 꽤 비싼 것은 알고 있지?)

   B : Really? _____?
      (정말? 입장료가 얼만데?)

   2 A : I will go get the tickets. (내가 티켓 사올게.)

   B : Okay, I need to sit down for awhile. _____.
      (알았어. 난 조금 앉아 있어야겠어. 다리가 너무 아프다.)

2. Tapping

   • pricey : 비싸다
   • admission : 입장(료)

3. Pattern

   이 숙제가 날 골치 아프게 한다.

   (This homework) is killing me.

🖥 과제 작문 연습

   Key phrase를 가지고 두 사람이 대화를 하는 상황을 만들어 보세요.

   Key phrase : **My feet are killing me.**

* Universal Studios Hollywood (할리우드 유니버설 스튜디오)

Universal Studios Hollywood is one of the oldest and most famous American film studios still in continuous production. It is even nicknamed 'The Entertainment Capital of LA'. You can start with a tour of the studio's fabulous movie sets, where you may even catch a glimpse of a few of your favorite stars. Then move on to the amazing theme park, where you can try new attractions like 'Transformers : The Ride' as well as old favorites like 'Jurassic Park' and 'Water world'. Don't miss it!

할리우드는 아직까지 활발히 작품을 내는 가장 오래되고 유명한 미국 영화 촬영소이다. 할리우드는 'LA의 엔터테인먼트 수도'라고도 불린다. 할리우드에 가면 우선 스튜디오의 멋진 촬영 세트를 구경할 수 있고 운이 좋으면 당신이 좋아하는 스타도 볼 수 있다. 그런 다음 신나는 테마 놀이공원에 가면 '쥐라기 공원'과 '워터 월드' 같은 옛 놀이기구는 물론이고 '트랜스포머'와 같은 새로운 놀이기구도 타 볼 수 있다. 절대 놓치지 마라!

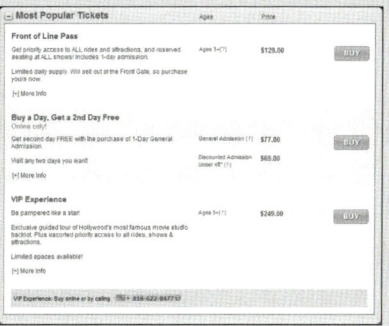

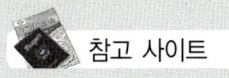
참고 사이트

* Universal Studios
http://www.universalstudioshollywood.com/

* The Ultimate Guide to Celebrities & Hollywood
http://www.seeing-stars.com/

Chapter 07

Review

🎧 Dialogue ✳

Yuna	Mike, I heard your job application for the US branch has been accepted.
Mike	You did? Did Mr. Smith tell you that?
Yuna	No, I overheard him. Oh, speak of the devil – here he comes.
Smith	Congratulations! You are both being transferred to the overseas branch.
Yuna	Wow, I got the spot! What am I going to need?
Smith	For starters, a passport, a working visa and an international driver's license.

Comprehension Questions

1. **Who is NOT being transferred to the US?**

   a. Yuna

   b. Mike

   c. Mr. Smith

   d. Mike and Yuna

   HINT You are both being transferred to the overseas branch.

2. **How did Yuna know she was being transferred?**

   a. Mr. Smith told her.

   b. She overheard Mr. Smith.

   c. She made a guess.

   d. She asked other colleagues.

   HINT Congratulations! You are both being transferred to the overseas branch.

Dialogue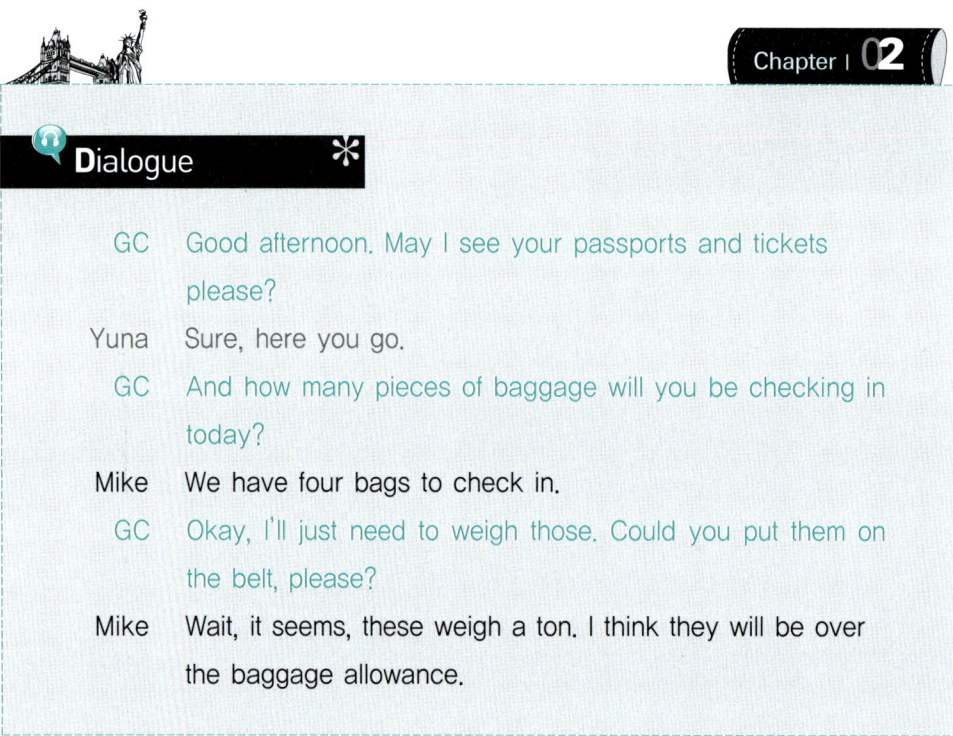

GC   Good afternoon. May I see your passports and tickets please?

Yuna   Sure, here you go.

GC   And how many pieces of baggage will you be checking in today?

Mike   We have four bags to check in.

GC   Okay, I'll just need to weigh those. Could you put them on the belt, please?

Mike   Wait, it seems, these weigh a ton. I think they will be over the baggage allowance.

Comprehension Questions

1. What does the ground crew want to do with the bags?

    a. check for dangerous items

    b. weigh the bags

    c. check the color of the bags

    d. put name tags on the bags

    HINT   Okay, I'll just need to weigh those. Could you put them on the belt, please?

2. What does 'weigh a ton' mean in the dialogue?

    a. The bags are oversized.

    b. A ton needs to be weighed.

    c. The bags weigh about 0.1 kilos.

    d. The bags are very heavy.

    HINT   Wait, it seems, these weigh a ton. I think they will be over the baggage allowance.

 Chapter I **03**

Dialogue ✳

(IA : Immigration Agent)

IA May I see your passport please? What is the purpose of your visit? I mean, what brings you to America?

Yuna Well, I am here to take a language program at UCLA. Thanks to my company.

IA Wow. That's a top notch school. Then, where are you going to stay?

Yuna Well, for the time being, I'll be at the youth hostel.

IA Okay, Good luck with your program. Enjoy the California sunshine.

Yuna Thank you.

Comprehension Questions

1. **What is the reason for Yuna's visit?**

   a. She is planning to study at UCLA.

   b. She is going to work at UCLA.

   c. She is visiting her friends at UCLA.

   d. She has a conference at UCLA.

   HINT Well, I am here to take a language program at UCLA.

2. **Which word does NOT have the same meaning as 'top notch'?**

   a. prestigious   b. high ranked

   c. oldest   d. excellent

   HINT Wow. That's a top notch school.

Chapter 04

Dialogue ✳

Mike	Geez, I need to ask someone for directions. Oh, there's a gas station.
W	Afternoon. You want regular or diesel?
Mike	Actually, umm... We're not here to fill up the gas. How do I get to 'Universal Studios'?
W	Go straight; hang a left at the first corner and you'll see a pizza place.
Mike	OK, what's next?
W	Just follow the signs with the big globe that say 'Universal'. You can't miss it.

Comprehension Questions

1. Where does Mike stop to ask for directions?

   a. The gas station

   b. A pizza restaurant

   c. Universal Studios

   d. On the corner

   HINT Oh, there's a gas station.

2. Where should Mike turn left?

   a. when he sees the 'Universal Studios' signs

   b. when he finds the pizza place

   c. when he drives out the gas station

   d. when he is at the first corner

   HINT Hang a left at the first corner and you'll see a pizza place.

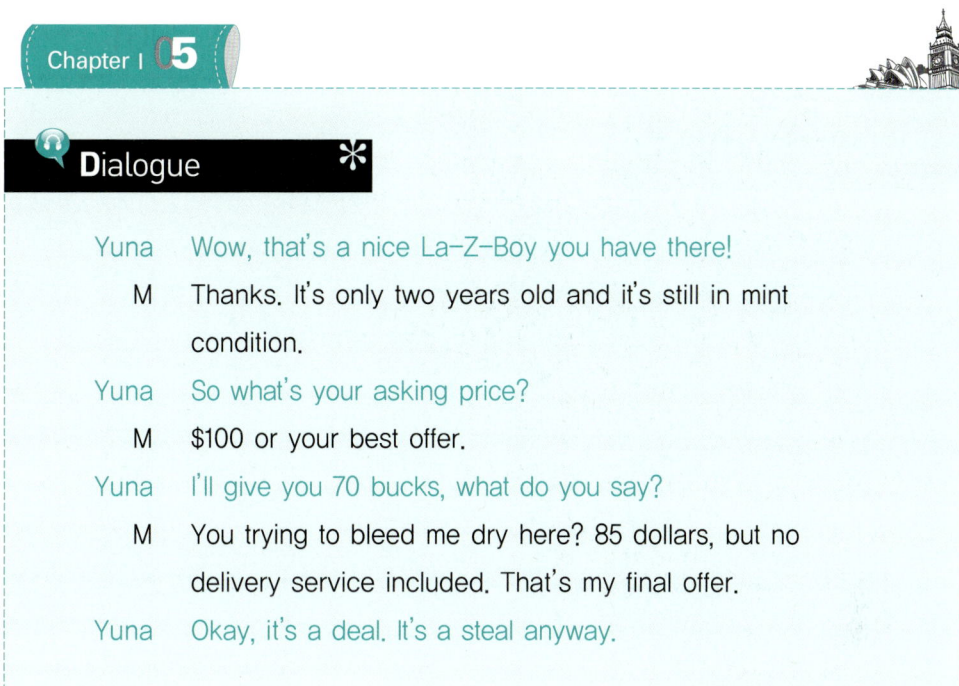

Dialogue ✳

Yuna Wow, that's a nice La-Z-Boy you have there!

M Thanks. It's only two years old and it's still in mint condition.

Yuna So what's your asking price?

M $100 or your best offer.

Yuna I'll give you 70 bucks, what do you say?

M You trying to bleed me dry here? 85 dollars, but no delivery service included. That's my final offer.

Yuna Okay, it's a deal. It's a steal anyway.

Comprehension Questions

1. **What is the condition of the La-Z-Boy?**

   a. brand new   b. in extremely good shape

   c. full of scratches   d. very old

   HINT It's only two years old and it's still in mint condition.

2. **How much of a discount did Yuna get?**

   a. 10 dollars   b. 15 dollars

   c. 30 dollars   d. 70 dollars

   HINT $100 or your best offer... 85 dollars, but no delivery service included.

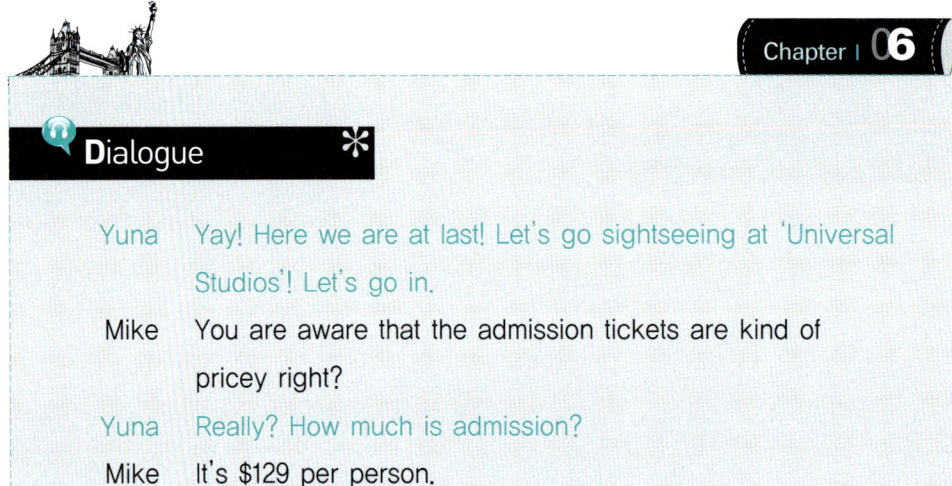

Chapter 06

Dialogue ✳

Yuna Yay! Here we are at last! Let's go sightseeing at 'Universal Studios'! Let's go in.

Mike You are aware that the admission tickets are kind of pricey right?

Yuna Really? How much is admission?

Mike It's $129 per person.

Yuna I'm sure it's worth it.

Mike Okay, you go get the tickets. I need to sit down for awhile. My feet are killing me.

Comprehension Questions

1. Yuna does not want to go in because the tickets are expensive.

   a. True
   b. False

   HINT I'm sure it's worth it.

2. What is Mike going to do next?

   a. He will look for a place to sit.
   b. He will buy the admission tickets.
   c. He will go to the hospital.
   d. He will park his car.

   HINT I need to sit down for awhile. My feet are killing me.

1. For _____, you should do some warm up exercise before swimming.

   a. start
   b. starters
   c. starting
   d. started

   HINT '시작으로'라는 연어 표현

2. I heard he will be _____ to the headquarters.

   a. transferred
   b. phone
   c. move
   d. changed

   HINT 본사로 옮겨지다. will be+pp 형태

3. It's good to acquire an international _____ before you leave Korea.

   a. drivers license
   b. drive maintenance
   c. driver's ID card
   d. drive certificate

   HINT 국제 운전면허증

4. _____ forms are over at that counter.

   a. Apply
   b. Applicable
   c. Applying
   d. Application

   HINT 지원서 양식

5. How many _____ of baggage will you be checking in?

   a. piece

   b. kilos

   c. pieces

   d. slices

   HINT   baggage 양사

6. The bags are over the _____. They should be below 20kgs.

   a. limited

   b. overweight bags

   c. travel bags

   d. baggage allowance

   HINT   수화물 허용량

7. Please _____ this jar on the shelf.

   a. place with

   b. put

   c. position out

   d. takes

   HINT   ~을 ~에 놓다

8. The most important _____ of this promotion is to increase sales.

   a. situation

   b. intend

   c. essential

   d. purpose

   HINT   프로모션의 목적

9. Harvard is one of the _____ schools in America.

    a. most prettiest

    b. top notch

    c. high teaching

    d. pristine

    HINT '최고의' 라는 뜻을 가진 표현 찾기

10. Keep an eye on my bag for _____.

    a. the time being

    b. my house

    c. on purpose

    d. sale

    HINT 잠시 동안

11. He _____ up the room with balloons this morning.

    a. filled

    b. backed

    c. stay

    d. filed

    HINT 채우다. this morning – 과거형

12. Go straight and you will see a signal that tells you to _____ right.

    a. skip to

    b. traverse

    c. hang a

    d. pound

    HINT '오른쪽으로 돌다' 라는 표현 찾기

13. I am _____ President Obama on Twitter.

    a. follow
    b. follow to
    c. follow with
    d. following

    HINT '따르고 있다' → 〈be 동사+ⓥ-ing+목적어〉

14. Give me your best and final _____ for this table.

    a. acceptance
    b. finalize
    c. offer
    d. propose

    HINT 마지막 제안 가격

15. Secretary-general Ban _____ a speech at the UN conference last week.

    a. make
    b. delivered
    c. present
    d. transported

    HINT 연설을 하다. last week – 과거형

16. _____ it's a steal, I will take ten pairs of these.

    a. Since
    b. Because of
    c. However
    d. Therefore

    HINT It's a steal=값이 매우 싸다. '값이 매우 싸기 때문에 10켤레 사겠다.'

17. They are somewhat conservative _____ we are on the liberal side.

    a. because of

    b. due to

    c. whereas

    d. after all

    HINT 그들은 보수적인 쪽에 있는 반면에 우리는 진보적인 쪽에 있다.

18. _____ the weather is good, we will go camping.

    a. As long as

    b. Besides

    c. In case of

    d. Along with

    HINT 날씨가 좋으면 캠핑을 가겠다.

19. This dress is too _____. I cannot afford it.

    a. filled

    b. pricey

    c. inexpensive

    d. off season

    HINT I cannot afford it. 그것을 구매할 형편이 안 된다.

20. That _____ sized pizza is not big enough for me.

    a. large

    b. abnormal

    c. hasty

    d. petite

    HINT not big enough : 충분히 크지 않다 → 작다

Chapter 08

Opening a Bank Account

Topic	Opening a Bank Account
Summary	Yuna has trouble withdrawing money at the ATM from her domestic bank account. She tries to open a new bank account in the States.

주제	은행에서 새 계좌 열기
줄거리	유나는 국내 카드로 현금지급기에서 현금을 빼려고 하는데 문제가 생겼다. 그녀는 미국 은행에서 계좌를 새로 열려고 한다.

Pre-check Quiz ✻

Q. 다음 중 의미 설명이 틀린 것을 고르시오.

a. withdraw – 입금
b. ATM – 현금지급기
c. domestic card – 국내 카드
d. overseas – 해외

Dialogue ✻

Yuna   Hi, I can't withdraw money from the ATM with this card. What's wrong?

Teller   Oh I see. This is a domestic card. It cannot be used overseas.

Yuna   Then do I need to open an account here?

Teller   Yes. It's very simple. Just fill out this form and show me two forms of ID.

Yuna   I have a passport and a student ID.

Teller   That's the ticket.

- -

유나   안녕하세요. 이 카드로 현금지급기에서 돈을 인출할 수 없어서요. 뭐가 문제죠?

텔러   아. 이 카드는 국내 카드입니다. 해외에서는 사용할 수 없습니다.

유나   그럼 여기서 새로운 계좌를 열어야 하나요?

텔러   네, 과정은 매우 간단합니다. 이 서류를 작성해주시고 신분증 2개만 보여주시면 돼요.

유나   여권과 학생증이 있습니다.

텔러   그거면 좋습니다.

01 Comprehension Questions

1. Yuna couldn't withdraw money from the ATM because _____.

   a. she didn't bring her credit card

   b. she used her domestic card

   c. the ATM was infected by a virus

   d. the ATM was out of service

   HINT This is a domestic card. It cannot be used overseas.

2. Which two forms of ID did Yuna present?

   a. passport and student ID

   b. passport

   c. driver's license and student ID.

   d. driver's license and ATM card

   HINT I have a passport and a student ID.

02 Vocabulary

1. withdraw money : 돈을 인출하다

   ↔ deposit : 입금 (make a deposit : 입금하다)

2. ATM : 현금인출기

   Automated Teller Machine

3. domestic / overseas card : 국내 / 해외 카드

   This is a domestic card. It cannot be used overseas.

4. fill out the form : 서류를 작성하다

   Just fill out this form and show me two forms of ID.

5. ID : 신분증(주민등록증)

   Identification

1. **I cannot withdraw money from the ATM.** 현금지급기에서 돈을 인출할 수가 없다.

표현설명

=I cannot get money from the machine.
withdraw(=take out money)
to withdraw things or to withdraw yourself

상황

Yuna : Hi, I cannot withdraw money from the ATM with this card. What's wrong?
(안녕하세요. 이 카드로 현금지급기에서 돈을 인출할 수 없어서요. 뭐가 문제죠?)

Teller : Oh I see. This is a domestic card. It cannot be used overseas.
(아, 이 카드는 국내 카드입니다. 해외에서는 사용할 수 없습니다.)

응용문제

Amy : You said you would pay back that 50 bucks.
(너 빌린 50불 갚는다고 했잖아.)

Liam : I tried but _____.
(돈 빼려고 했는데 현금지급기가 작동하지 않아.)

2. **Do I need to open an account here?** 여기서 새 계좌를 열어야 하나요?

표현설명

=Is it necessary to create a new account at this bank?
We use the terms 'open' and 'close' when discussing accounts.

상황

Yuna : Then do I need to open an account here?
(그럼 여기서 새로운 계좌를 열어야 하나요?)

Teller : Yes. It's very simple. Just fill out this form and show me two forms of ID.
(네, 과정은 매우 간단합니다. 이 서류를 작성해주시고 신분증 2개만 보여주시면 돼요.)

Teller : Do you have an account here? (저희 은행에 계좌가 있으세요?)

Student : No, I just arrived yesterday. _____.

(아니요. 어제 도착해서 없어요. 여기서 새로운 계좌를 열고 싶어요.)

3. **That's the ticket./Just the ticket.** 그거면 됩니다./안성맞춤입니다.

표현설명

'That's the ticket.' is often used to express confirmation.
It is used to show something that is needed in a specific situation.

상황

Yuna : I have a passport and a student ID. (여권과 학생증이 있습니다.)

Teller : That's the ticket. (그거면 좋습니다.)

응용문제 1

This car could be _____ for a small family.
(이 자동차는 소가족에게 안성맞춤입니다.)

응용문제 2

Teacher : Class, I'd like someone to answer the question on the second page.
(여러분, 2페이지에 있는 질문에 답하시기 바랍니다.)

Student : The answer is Karl Marx, right? (답이 칼 막스 맞죠?)

Teacher : Yes, _____! (네, 정답입니다!)

1. Basic

Fill out ~. (~을 작성하여 주십시오.)

1 나 이력서 작성했어.

_____

2 나 삼성전기에 넣을 입사 지원서 작성했어.

_____

3 입시 원서를 작성하시면 제가 인쇄해 드리겠습니다.

_____

2. One Step Further

Why don't you ~ ? (정중한 요청 : ~해 주시겠습니까?)

1 이 설문지를 작성해 주시겠습니까?

_____

2 혼인신고서를 작성해 주시겠습니까?

_____

3 이 서류를 작성해 주시겠습니까?

_____

05 TOEIC 실전 문제 풀이

1. You can withdraw money from the _____ over there.

   a. bank
   b. cash machine
   c. secured loan
   d. a truck of money

   HINT ATM = Automated Teller Machine(현금자동인출기)의 동의어 찾기

2. We need to check your _____ in order to sell you alcohol.

   a. identification card
   b. cell phone number
   c. student number
   d. ideal card

   HINT ID = 신분증

3. Would you fill _____ the form below?

   a. on
   b. at
   c. with
   d. out

   HINT 전치사에 따른 다른 의미를 인지한다.

06 Auto-Memorization

1. withdraw money : 출금하다

   Withdraw money from the ATM.

2. ATM : 현금 자동 입출금기

   ATM card

3. domestic/overseas card : 국내/국제 카드

   This card is a domestic card.

4. fill out the form : 서식을 작성하다

   Just fill out the form.

5. ID : 신분증

   Give me 2 pieces of ID.

1. 연상 퀴즈

1 A : Here's the card. I think it's better for you to take my card with you.
(카드 여기 있다. 아무래도 내 카드를 가져가는 게 나을 것 같아.)

B : Thanks mom, but this is a _____. I can't use it overseas.
(고마워요 엄마. 그렇지만 이건 국내 카드라서 해외에서 사용 가능하지 않아요.)

2 A : Good afternoon. May I help you? (안녕하세요. 무엇을 도와드릴까요?)

B : Yes. I lost my _____ card a week ago. I came here to request another.
(안녕하세요. 1주일 전 제 신분증을 잃어버렸는데 다시 신청하려고 왔습니다.)

2. Tapping

- ATM : 현금 자동 입출금기
- withdraw money : 출금하다
- fill out the form : 서식을 작성하다

3. Pattern

나는 양식을 작성했어.

I filled (the form) out.

Fill out (the form).

과제 작문 연습

Key phrase를 가지고 두 사람이 대화를 하는 상황을 만들어 보세요.

Key phrase : **Do I need to open an account here?**

 Culture Tip

* 미국 도시에 있는 은행에는 한국인 직원이 있어 한국어로 은행 업무를 도와준다. 그리고 몇몇 ATM 기기들은 한국어로 설정이 가능하니, 미국에서의 은행 방문을 두려워하지 않아도 된다.

a. Press the card to insert it into the ATM. 현금지급기에 카드를 넣으세요.

b. Please enter your pin number. 비밀번호를 누르세요.

c. Press an arrow key to select an option.
거래하고자 하는 항목 옆 화살표 버튼을 누르세요.

관련어휘
- Cash=현금 지급
- Printed Balance=잔고 출력
- Cash with Receipt=현금거래 및 영수증
- Balance on Screen=잔액 조회
- Change Pin Number=비밀번호 변경
- Print Mini Statement=최근 입출금 표 출력

  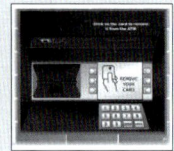

d. Press the arrow key next to the required amount.
원하는 금액 옆에 있는 화살표 버튼을 누르세요.

e. Please remove cash. 현금지급기에서 현금을 꺼내세요.

f. Remove your card. 카드를 꺼내세요.

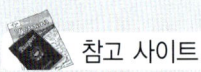 참고 사이트

* Bank of America
http://www.bankofamerica.com/

* 미국 한 번 못 가본 어느 스파이의 블로그 : 미국유학 – 은행계좌 만들기
http://americaspy.tistory.com/37

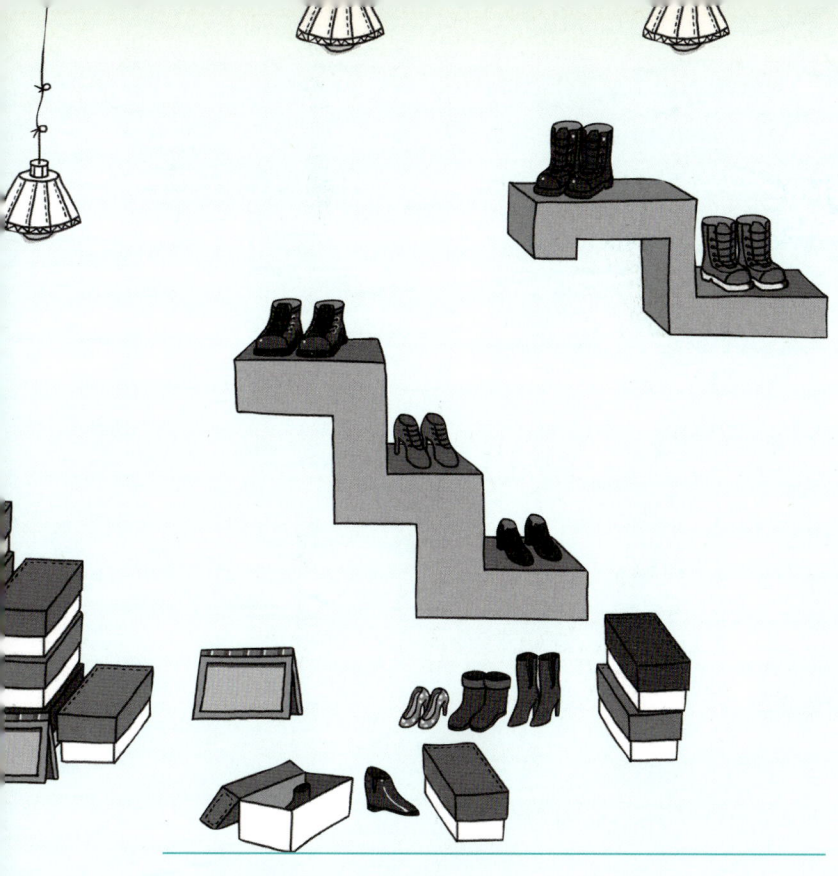

Chapter 09

Buying Shoes

Topic	Buying Shoes
Summary	Yuna is looking to buy a pair of pumps and Mike needs a pair of slippers. Yuna asks the clerk for some help.

주제	신발 구매하기
줄거리	유나는 펌프(3~5cm 굽의 편한 정장 구두)를 마이크는 슬리퍼를 장만하려고 한다. 유나는 직원에게 도움을 구한다.

Pre-check Quiz ✳

Q. 다음 중 의미 설명이 틀린 것을 고르시오.

a. practical – 실용적인

b. clearance sale – 창고 정리 세일

c. pumps – 운동 기계

d. wide – 볼이 넓은

🎧 Dialogue ✳

Yuna   Wow, that store is having a clearance sale. I need new shoes.

Mike   Me too. I could use a new pair of slippers.

(In the shoe store)

Yuna   Hi, I'm in the market for a practical pair of pumps. My size is 240.

Clerk   Pardon me but do you know the American size?

Yuna   Ah! Sorry. I think it is size 7.

Clerk   Here you are. They are 30% off today so they are $79. They are the hottest item.

Yuna   What a steal! I will take them.

유나   우와, 이 가게 창고 정리 세일한다. 나 새 신발이 필요했는데.

마크   나도. 새 슬리퍼를 샀으면 했어.

(신발 가게 안에서)

유나   안녕하세요. 실용적인 펌프 한 켤레 구매하러 왔습니다. 제 발 사이즈는 240이에요.

점원   실례합니다만 미국 사이즈를 아시나요?

유나   아! 죄송해요. 사이즈 7인 거 같아요.

점원   여기 있습니다. 오늘은 30% 할인되어 79달러입니다. 제일 잘 팔리는 상품이죠.

유나   진짜 싸네요! 사겠습니다.

01 Comprehension Questions

1. What is Yuna's American foot size?

   a. 245   b. 30

   c. 7   d. 79

   HINT I think it is size 7.

2. What does it mean when Yuna says, "I will take them."?

   a. I'll reserve the shoes.

   b. I will steal the shoes.

   c. I'll give them to someone else.

   d. I'll buy the shoes.

   HINT What a steal! I will take them.

02 Vocabulary

1. clearance sale : 창고 정리 세일(=garage sale)

   That store is having a clearance sale.

2. pair of slippers / pumps : 슬리퍼/펌프 한 켤레

   (pair : 두 쪽이 한 켤레) one pair of shoes, two pairs of shoes

   I'm in the market for a practical pair of pumps.

3. practical : 실용적인

   실용 영어(practical English), 실용 화학(practical chemistry),

   실용 예술(practical art)

4. (30%) off : (30%) 할인(=30% discount=reduced by 30%)

   They are 30% off today.

5. hottest item : 가장 잘 팔리는 상품

   They are the hottest item. → They sell like hot cakes.

1. **I could use a new pair of slippers.** 새 슬리퍼 한 켤레 있었으면 좋겠다.

   표현설명

   Mike is saying, "I wasn't searching for new slippers but I do need some."

   상황

   Yuna : Wow, that store is having a clearance sale. I need new shoes.
           (우와, 이 가게 창고 정리 세일한다. 나 새 신발이 필요했는데.)

   Mike : Me too. I could use a new pair of slippers. (나도. 새 슬리퍼를 샀으면 했어.)

   응용문제

   Alan   : I'm going to the mall. Do you want anything? (나 몰에 가는데 너 뭐 필요해?)

   Melissa : _____. (새 슬리퍼 한 켤레 있었으면 좋겠다.)

2. **I'm in the market for a practical pair of pumps.**

   실용적인 펌프 한 켤레 사러 시장에 왔다.

   표현설명

   = I want to buy a practical pair of pumps.

   [I am looking for/I want/I would like] is the same as making a request.

   used typically to express something that you must shop or search for

   상황

   Yuna : Hi, I'm in the market for a practical pair of pumps. My size is 240.
           (안녕하세요. 실용적인 펌프 한 켤레 구매하러 왔습니다. 제 발 사이즈는 240이에요.)

   Clerk : Pardon me, but do you know the American size?
           (실례합니다만, 미국 사이즈를 아시나요?)

   응용문제

   Max   : Hello Julia! What are you doing here? (줄리아 안녕! 너 여기서 뭐해?)

   Julia : Hey! _____. (안녕! 실용적인 펌프 한 켤레 사러 시장 왔어.)

1. Basic

I'm in ~ to ~. (나는 ~에 ~을 하기 위해 왔다.)

1 저는 이 학교에 영어를 배우러 왔습니다.

I'm in _____ to _____.

2 저는 김 교수님의 리더십을 배우기 위해 이 프로젝트에 참여하게 되었습니다.

I'm in _____ to _____.

3 저는 Brown을 만나 뵈러 이 빌딩에 왔습니다.

I'm in _____ to _____.

2. One Step Further

Are you here to ~? (너 여기에 ~을 하러 왔니?)

1 너 신발 사러 여기 왔니?

_____

2 너 사은품 받으러 여기 왔니?

_____

3 강의하러 오셨나요?

_____

05 TOEIC 실전 문제 풀이

1. We can buy secondhand goods at _____.

   a. season off sale   b. garbage sale

   c. shopping plaza   d. swap meet

   HINT Flea market＝Swap meet

2. That pair of slippers is 50% _____.

   a. drop   b. offline

   c. discounted   d. on

   HINT off＝discounted

3. The hat is one of the _____ this season.

   a. hottest items   b. better items

   c. hot item   d. leisure items

   HINT one of the + 최상급

06 Auto-Memorization

1. clearance sale : 창고 정리 세일

   Wow, that store is having a clearance sale.

2. pair of slippers/pumps : 슬리퍼/펌프 신발 한 켤레

   I could use a new pair of slippers.

3. (30%) off : (30%) 세일

   They are 30% off today so they are $79.

4. hottest item : 제일 잘 나가는 물건

   They are the hottest item [in the shop/in the city/this week/this year].

5. practical : 실용적인

   I'm in the market for a practical pair of pumps.

1. 연상 퀴즈

1 A : Happy birthday Susan! Here's your birthday present. Do you like it?
(생일 축하해 수잔! 여기 생일 선물. 어때, 맘에 들어?)

B : Oh wow, this scheduler is both _____ and pretty. Thank you!
(어머나, 이 스케줄러는 실용적이면서도 예쁘다. 고마워!)

2 A : What's on the website? It seems like you're going to jump right in there.
(웹사이트에 뭐가 있어? 너 거기로 빨려 들어갈 것 같아.)

B : Hey, my favorite Gucci bag is _____ and I'm participating in an auction now.
(안녕. 지금 내가 좋아하는 구찌 백이 90% 세일을 하고 있어서 그 경매에 참가 중이야.)

2. Tapping

- hottest item : 제일 잘 나가는 물건
- clearance sale : 정리 세일
- practical : 실용적인

3. Pattern Practice

저는 장을 보러 슈퍼마켓에 왔습니다.

I'm in (the supermarket) to (grocery shop).

과제 작문 연습

Key phrase를 가지고 두 사람이 대화를 하는 상황을 만들어 보세요.

Key phrase : **I'm in the market for a practical pair of pumps.**

 Culture Tip

* 베버리힐즈

캘리포니아 서남부에 있는 도시로 LA에 둘러싸여 있으나, LA와는 완전히 별개의 행정 구역이다.
베벌리 힐즈는 할리우드 유명 배우들이 사는 것으로 유명하며, 인근엔 로데오 거리(Rodeo
drive)라는 쇼핑 밀집 지역이 있으며 이곳은 관광 명소이기도 하다. 명동보다도 작은 곳이지만 명
품 브랜드 건물이 많이 입점해 있는 것으로 유명하다.

* 신발 사이즈 표

한국 (mm)	미국 (U.S.A)		영국 (U.K)		유럽 (EURO)	
	MEN	WOMEN	MEN	WOMEN	MEN	WOMEN
220	–	5	–	2.5	–	35.5
225	–	5.5	–	3	–	36
230	–	6	–	3.5	–	36.5
235	–	6.5	–	4	–	37.5
240	6	7	5	4.5	38.5	38
245	6.5	7.5	5.5	5	39	38.5
250	7	8	6	5.5	40	39
255	7.5	8.5	6.5	6	40.5	40
260	8	9	7	6.5	41	40.5
265	8.5	9.5	7.5	7	42	41
270	9	10	8	7.5	42.5	42
275	9.5	10.5	8.5	8	43	42.5
280	10	11	9	8.5	44.5	43
285	10.5	11.5	9.5	9	45	44
290	11	12	10	9.5	45.5	44.5
295	11.5	–	10.5	–	46	–
300	12	–	11	–	46.5	–
305	12.5	–	11.5	–	47	–
310	13	–	12	–	47.5	–

 참고 사이트

* Jumble Sale에 대한 사전적 의미 및 동의어
http://en.wikipedia.org/wiki/Rummage_sale

Chapter 10

Going to the
Supermarket

Topic	Going to the Supermarket
Summary	Mike and Yuna are going to the supermarket to buy ingredients they need in order to make a special dinner.

주제	슈퍼마켓에 가기
줄거리	마이크와 유나는 특별한 저녁 식사를 만들기 위해 필요한 재료를 사러 수퍼마켓에 간다.

Pre-check Quiz ✳

Q. 다음 중 의미 설명이 틀린 것을 고르시오.

a. check out − 나가다

b. in total − 완전히

c. expire − 만료되다

d. not my day − 내 날이 아니다

Dialogue ✳

Yuna	I am tired of grocery shopping. Didn't we get everything we need?
Mike	Yup, that's about it. Now, we can go to the checkout.

(Beep beep beep)

Cashier	That'll be 45 dollars in total.
Mike	Oh wait, can I use this coupon?
Cashier	I am sorry but we can't accept it. It expired yesterday.
Mike	Today is just not my day.

유나	나 장보는 데 지쳤어. 우리 필요한 거 다 넣었지?
마이크	응, 우리 이제 계산하러 가자.

(삡, 삡, 삡)

캐셔	총 45 달러입니다.
마이크	아, 잠시만요. 이 쿠폰 사용할 수 있나요?
캐셔	죄송하지만 못 받습니다. 어제가 만료일이었어요.
마이크	오늘은 제 날이 아닌가 봐요.

Comprehension Questions

1. Why can't Mike and Yuna use their coupon?

   a. Because Yuna lost it.

   b. the clerk

   c. Because their coupon is outdated.

   HINT Oh I'm sorry. This coupon expired last week.

2. Where do Mike and Yuna go once they've picked out all their groceries?

   a. To check their total

   b. To the checkout

   c. After finishing food shopping

   HINT Yup, that's about it. Now, we can go to the checkout.

02 Vocabulary

1. grocery shopping : 시장보기

   (used when a person is shopping for food items)

2. checkout : 계산대 / check out : 나가다

   (used when a customer/shopper has completed their shopping and is now ready to exchange money for the items they have selected)

3. in total : 총 합계 (=the final amount or cost of your groceries)

   There are 7 rooms on the 1st floor of the hotel and 7 rooms on the 2nd floor. The hotel has 14 rooms in total.

4. expire : 만료되다, 만기되다 (=come to an end or complete something)

1. **Didn't we get everything we need?** 필요한 것 다 샀지?

표현설명

Grocery shopping is shopping that is done on a 'needs' basis.
(meaning you only go shopping for groceries when you need food)

상황

Yuna : I am tired of grocery shopping. Didn't we get everything we need?
(나 장보는 데 지쳤어. 우리 필요한 거 다 넣었지?)

Mike : Yup, that's about it. Now, we can go to the checkout. (응, 우리 이제 계산하러 가자.)

응용문제

Mother : Did you get sugar, milk, and eggs to make shortbread?
(우리 쇼트브래드 만들 때 필요한 설탕, 우유, 계란 구했니?)

Son : Sure. I got it all, just like you asked. (네. 말씀하신 대로 다 구했어요.)

Mother : Then _____. (그럼 필요한 거 다 샀다.)

2. **We can go to the checkout.** 우리 계산대로 가야겠다.

표현설명

Once shopping is completed; customers will go to 'the checkout'. As a noun 'the checkout' is a station where a cashier waits to help the customer/shopper exchange the items they have selected for money. Once the cashier announces the total amount and accepts the money, check-out is complete.

상황

Yuna : I am tired of grocery shopping. Didn't we get everything we need?
(나 장보는데 지쳤어. 우리 필요한 거 다 넣었지?)

Mike : Yup, that's about it. Now, we can go to the checkout.
(응, 우리 이제 계산하러 가자.)

Monica : Did you get the butter? (버터는 찾았니?)

Jack : Oh, how many times do I have to tell you? I got it all!

(아, 몇 번이나 말해야 되니? 이미 다 구했다니까.)

Monica : OK, OK. _____.

(알았어, 알았어. 우리 계산하러 가자.)

3. It expired yesterday. 어제 만료되었다.

'expired' is a term used to show completion and that the item is no longer usable. 'It expired yesterday.' or 'It expired two weeks ago.' means that it can no longer be used.

Mike : Oh wait, can I use this coupon? (아, 잠시만요. 이 쿠폰 사용할 수 있나요?)

Cashier : I am sorry but we can't accept it. It expired yesterday.

(죄송하지만 못 받습니다. 어제가 만료일이었어요.)

Clara : Your total is $32.50. (총 $32.50입니다.)

Tom : Wait. I have a coupon for the detergent. (잠시만요. 이 세제 할인 쿠폰 있어요.)

Clara : Oh I'm sorry. _____.

(아, 죄송합니다. 어제 만료되었습니다.)

4. Today is just not my day. 오늘은 내 날이 아니다.

usually said after series of bad situations or disappointing circumstances

Cashier : I am sorry but we can't accept it. It expired yesterday.

(죄송하지만 못 받습니다. 어제가 만료일이었어요.)

Mike : Today is just not my day. (오늘은 제 날이 아닌가 봐요.)

Clerk : We are having a lucky draw event. Pick one.
(지금 행운 추첨을 하고 있습니다. 하나 뽑으세요.)

Mother : Oh no. It says 'Better luck next time.' I guess _____.
(안 돼. '다음 기회에'라고 써 있네요. 오늘은 제 날이 아닌가 봐요.)

04 Pattern Practice

1. Basic

I am sorry but ~. (부탁 : 죄송합니다 하지만 ~.)

1 미안하지만 TV 좀 꺼줄래?

I am sorry but _____?

2 미안하지만 빌린 돈 좀 돌려줄래?

I am sorry but _____?

3 미안하지만 잠깐 자리를 비워줄래? (전화 도중)

I am sorry but _____?

2. One Step Further

I am sorry but ~. (과거의 용서를 빌 때 : ~해서 미안합니다.)

1 너의 컵을 깨서 미안해.

I am sorry but _____.

2 수업을 빠져서 죄송해요.

I am sorry but _____.

3 과제를 안 해서 죄송합니다.

I am sorry but _____.

1. Three tomatoes, five bags of onions... It'll be $15 _____, ma'am.

   a. in total　　　　　　　b. in tall

   c. discount　　　　　　　d. in cash

   HINT 총계를 의미하는 표현이 나와야 한다.

2. The first _____ is only for buyers with less than 5 items.

   a. in cash　　　　　　　b. check stand

   c. calculate　　　　　　d. help desk

   HINT 뒤에 is는 be동사이므로 주어 역할을 해 줄 명사가 필요

3. This microwave's warranty has _____. You should pay for the repair from now on.

   a. expire　　　　　　　b. experienced

   c. run out　　　　　　　d. renewed

   HINT 현재 완료형인 have+pp

06 Auto-Memorization

1. grocery shopping : 시장보기

   I am tired of grocery shopping.

2. check out : 계산대, 나가다

   Now, we can go to the checkout.

3. in total : 총

   That will be 45 dollars in total.

4. expire : 만료되다, 만기되다

   It expired yesterday.

1. 연상 퀴즈

1 A : Mom, I need you to buy me a pair of new sneakers.
(엄마, 나 새 운동화가 필요해요.)

B : As soon as I finish the _____, I'll buy them.
(장 보고 난 후에 사줄게.)

2 A : Excuse me; do you know where the cash registers are?
(실례합니다, 혹시 계산대가 어디 있는지 아세요?)

B : Go to the 2nd floor to _____.
(나가시려면 2층으로 올라가세요.)

2. Tapping

• in total : 총

• expire : 만료되다, 만기되다

• check out : 나가다

3. Pattern Practice

미안하지만 너의 컵을 깼어.

I'm sorry but (I broke your cup).

📺 과제 작문 연습

Key phrase를 가지고 두 사람이 대화를 하는 상황을 만들어 보세요.

Key phrase : **Today is just not my day.**

* Manufacturer's coupon 제조회사 할인 쿠폰

America is a shopper's paradise with many types of coupon. These are the representative coupons that Americans usually use. You can find them almost anywhere – Sunday newspapers, local mailers and etc. The majority of manufacturer coupons have an expiration date stamped on them.

미국은 여러 종류의 쿠폰이 있는 쇼핑의 천국입니다. 좌측의 쿠폰은 미국인들이 평상시에 자주 사용하는 대표적인 쿠폰의 종류들입니다. 여러분은 이 쿠폰을 일간지, 지역 신문 등 거의 모든 곳에서 볼 수 있습니다. 대부분의 제조회사 할인 쿠폰은 유효기간이 찍혀 있습니다.

* Retailer's coupon 소매업자 쿠폰

It's a coupon that's usually attached on supermarket advertisement paper. It can discount the amount of total grocery bill, or a specific section of the store.

주로 슈퍼마켓 전단지에 붙어있는 쿠폰입니다. 소매업자 쿠폰을 사용하면 장을 본 총 구매액 혹은 매장의 특정구역 물품의 구매액을 할인받을 수 있습니다.

* Double coupon 더블 쿠폰

When the customer brings manufacturer's coupon and retailer's coupon, he can get the double discount of the total products.

더블 쿠폰은 구매자가 제조회사 할인 쿠폰과 소매업자 쿠폰을 가져올시, 총구매액에서 이중 할인을 받을 수 있게 하는 시스템입니다.

 참고 사이트

＊ 위키피디아 - 쿠폰의 종류
http://en.wikipedia.org/wiki/Coupon

＊ 쿠폰의 종류 이미지 파일 (Google)
http://www.google.com/images?hl=en&q=manufacturer%20coupon&wrapid=tlif12825394066
872&um=1&ie=UTF-8&source=og&sa=N&tab=wi

＊ 유튜브 채널
Grocery Shopping on a Budget - http://www.youtube.com/watch?v=q_ekh6s1xw0

＊ ESL Grocery Store Lesson
www.elcivics.com

＊ ESL 장보기 수업

Grocery stores sell food and other items like cards and flowers. Most people go the grocery store at least once a week. Grocery stores are usually in large one-story buildings. There are many parking spaces for cars in front of the buildings. Most grocery stores are open seven days a week.

슈퍼마켓에서는 음식, 카드, 꽃 등의 물품을 판매합니다. 대부분의 사람들은 일주일에 적어도 한 번은 마켓에 들릅니다. 슈퍼마켓은 대부분 커다란 단층 건물에 위치하고 있습니다. 건물 앞에는 커다란 주차장이 마련되어 있습니다. 거의 모든 슈퍼마켓은 하루도 빠짐없이 영업을 합니다.

＊ What is this? 이것은 무엇입니까?

· It is a shopping list. 이것은 구매 목록입니다.

· Before you go to the grocery store, it is a good idea to make a list. 장을 보러 가기 전 구매 목록을 작성하는 것도 좋은 생각입니다.

Chapter 11

Making **M**ovie **R**eservations
through the **Internet**

Topic	Making Movie Reservations through the Internet
Summary	Yuna and Mike are planning to watch a movie during the weekend. They are choosing the movie through the Internet.

주제	인터넷으로 영화 예매하기
줄거리	Yuna와 Mike는 주말에 영화를 볼 계획이다. 그들은 인터넷을 통해 영화를 고르고 있다.

Q. 다음 중 의미 설명이 틀린 것을 고르시오.

a. thriller — 공포 영화

b. nasty — 이상한

c. matinee — 마티니 칵테일

d. discount — 할인

Dialogue ✳

Yuna	I just logged in. Thriller, romantic comedy or action?
Mike	Actually, I like animations. How about *Toy Story*?
Yuna	Alrighty. There is regular, 3-D and 4D IMAX. Which one?
Mike	I don't like the 4D IMAX. I hate the chair shaking and all those nasty smells.
Yuna	OK then, the matinee or a late-night show?
Mike	Let's be early birds and catch the special discount.

유나	방금 로그인 했어. 공포 영화, 로맨틱 코미디, 액션 영화, 뭐 볼래?
마이크	사실 애니메이션이 보고 싶어. 토이 스토리 어때?
유나	그래. 일반, 3-D, 4D IMAX 있는데. 어떤 거?
마이크	나 4D IMAX는 안 좋아해. 의자 흔들리는 거랑 이상한 냄새 나는 것도 싫어.
유나	알았어. 그럼 조조 영화 아니면 심화 영화?
마이크	우리 아침 일찍 일어나서 특별 할인을 받자.

01 Comprehension Questions

1. What type of movie did Yuna and Mike decide to see?

   a. suspense   b. animation

   c. thriller   d. romantic comedy

   HINT Actually, I like animation. How about Toy Story?

2. Why doesn't Mike like the IMAX?

   a. He doesn't like the smells and special effects.

   b. He thinks it's boring.

   c. He doesn't like movies.

   d. He thinks they aren't very romantic.

   HINT I don't like the 4D IMAX. I hate the chair shaking and all those nasty smells.

02 Vocabulary

1. thriller : 스릴러/공포 영화

   a film/movie with scary and/or suspenseful themes

2. romantic comedy : 로맨틱 코미디

   a humorous film/movie with love and drama as its primary themes

3. R-rated movie(Restricted-rated) : 준 성인용 영화 (17세 이하는 부모 동반 시 관람)

   any genre(type) of film/movie that contains strong language, nudity, or violence

4. matinee : 조조 영화

   the early shows at the theater, opera or any type of artistic production with multiple day and evening show times

5. early birds : 부지런한 사람, 아침형 인간

   people who visit shopping malls, theaters and stores as early as possible to avoid crowds, get good seats and/or take advantage of special discounts

1. ## matinee or late night movie 조조 영화 아니면 심야 영화

표현설명

used to describe the times that movies will be shown during the days

상황

Yuna : OK then, the matinee or a late-night show?
(알았어. 그럼 조조 영화 아니면 심화 영화?)

Mike : Let's be early birds and catch the special discount.
(우리 일찍 일어나는 새가 되어 특별 할인을 받자.)

응용문제

Tom : Hey Meg, want to go see a movie? *Robin Hood* is playing at 9:30 p.m.
(메그, 영화 보러 갈래? 로빈 후드 9시 반에 상영한다.)

Meg : I can't make it that late.
(나 그렇게 늦은 시간은 안 돼.)

Tom : Okay, then we could see the _____ instead of a _____.
(알았어. 그럼 심야 영화 대신 조조 영화 보면 되지 뭐.)

2. ## There is the normal feature, 3-D(dimensional) and 4D IMAX(Image Maximum). 일반 영화, 3-D 영화와 4-D 아이맥스

표현설명

Ways a film might be viewed. A normal feature is the standard movie viewing option.

상황

Yuna : Alrighty. There is regular, 3-D and 4D IMAX. Which one?
(그래. 일반, 3-D, 4D IMAX 있는데. 어떤 거?)

Mike : I don't like the 4D IMAX. I hate the chair shaking and all those nasty smells.
(나 4D IMAX는 안 좋아해. 의자 흔들리는 거랑 이상한 냄새 나는 것도 싫어.)

Caroline : Did you see *Avatar*?
(너 아바타 봤니?)

Abigail : I did. I actually saw it at the _____.
(응. 사실 아이맥스 4D로 봤어.)

Caroline : Oh, well I don't like all those fancy effects. I just saw the _____.
(아, 난 그런 특수 효과들 싫더라. 난 그냥 일반 버전으로 봤어.)

3. Let's be the early birds and catch the special discounts.

아침에 일찍 가면 특별 할인을 받는다.

표현설명

A very common phrase used to prove the benefits of getting up early in the morning

상황

Yuna : OK then, the matinee or a late-night show?
(알았어. 그럼 조조 영화 아니면 심화 영화?)

Mike : Let's be early birds and catch the special discount.
(우리 아침 일찍 일어나서 특별 할인을 받자.)

응용문제

Walter : What are you doing tomorrow?
(너 내일 뭐하니?)

Jason : You know, the electronics store is having a laptop sale. But it's first come first served.
(너 그거 아니? 전자 제품 가게에서 노트북 컴퓨터 세일하고 있대. 하지만 선착순이래.)

Walter : _____.
(그럼 우리 일찍 일어나서 그 노트북을 사수하자.)

1. Basic

How about ~ ? (제안 : ~은 어때?) cf.(대답) → OK / I am sorry but ~.

1 오늘 밤 술 한잔 어때?

How about _____?

2 오늘밤 여자 헌팅하러 갈래?

How about _____?

3 아이 쇼핑 어때?

How about _____?

2. One Step Further

What do you think about ~ ? (구체적 답을 구하는 의견 묻기 : ~은 어때?)

1 이 맥주 맛 어때? 거품이 빠진 거 같지 않니?

What do you think about _____? Isn't it too flat?

2 애피타이저 맛이 어때?

What do you think about _____?

3 그 영화 결말이 어떤 거 같니?

What do you think about _____?

05 TOEIC 실전 문제 풀이

1. I know you don't like thriller movies, _____ it's my birthday today. Let's watch it.

   a. but
   b. so
   c. and
   d. therefore

   HINT 두 문장을 이어주는 접속사가 필요

2. Don't you dare try to watch _____ movie alone! You're only 15.

   a. child
   b. R-rated
   c. PG 13
   d. PG

   HINT 상황 속 아이는 15살임

3. Sam is an _____. He never puts off the work he has to do.

   a. early bird
   b. narrow-minded
   c. sensitive
   d. earnest

   HINT an이 들어간 후엔 모음 단어가 따라옴

06 Auto-Memorization

1. thriller : 스릴러 장르

   Thriller, romantic comedy or R-rated movie?

2. romantic comedy : 로맨틱 코미디 장르

3. R-rated movie : 19세 이상 관람가

4. Matinee : 조조 영화

   OK, then matinee or late-night movie?

5. early birds : 부지런한 사람

   Let's be early birds and catch the special discounts.

1. 연상 퀴즈

1 A : What is your favorite movie genre, Sophie?

(소피, 네가 제일 좋아하는 영화 장르는 뭐니?)

B : _____. They are easy to watch.

(로맨틱 코미디. 가볍게 볼 수 있잖아.)

2 A : Hey, are you watching the '*Phantom of the Opera*' tonight?

(이봐, 너 밤에 '오페라의 유령' 보러 가니?)

B : No, I'm going to the _____ show. It's much cheaper that way.

(아니, 조조로 볼 거야. 이렇게 보는 게 훨씬 더 싸거든.)

2. Tapping

- showtime : 상영작 소개
- R-rated movie : 19세 이상 관람가
- early bird : 부지런한 사람

3. Pattern Practice

아이 쇼핑 어때?

How about (window shopping)?

🖥 과제 작문 연습

Key phrase를 가지고 두 사람이 대화를 하는 상황을 만들어 보세요.

Key phrase : **Let's be early birds and catch the special discount.**

 Culture Tip

※ Total Enterainment

LA is known internationally as the film capital of the world and is home to the top movie theatres out there. In recent years, such theatres are not just where the movies are screened and seen but have been transformed into a space of 'Total Entertainment'. To say that such multiplexes are sought after only by moviegoers to view a selection of a few films would be an understatement. These are images only found in the past. For the multiplexes of today provide much more than a movie but act as a one stop entertainment center where people can enjoy a weekend by waiting at a tea shop before show time, watching the movie followed by dinner in a restaurant and ending the date with a cocktail in a bar that stays open late.

영화산업의 수도 LA에는 국제적으로 명성이 높은 극장들이 곳곳에 있습니다. 최근 들어 일부 극장들은 영화만을 상영하는 곳이 아닌 '토털 엔터테인먼트' 장소로 탈바꿈하고 있습니다. 그저 멀티플렉스(multiflex)를 갖추고 여러 개의 영화만을 상영하면 관객이 찾아온다는 것은 이제 옛말이 되었고, 주말이면 극장 내에서 연인과 라이브밴드 공연을 보고 커피숍에서 차를 마시다가 영화를 관람하고 극장에 있는 고급 레스토랑에서 식사를 한 다음, 분위기 있는 바(bar)에서 칵테일을 밤 늦도록 즐길 수 있는 곳이 바로 요즘 문을 열고 있는 토털 엔터테인먼트 극장입니다.

With Director Hall theatre seats 2 feet from the screen and made of leather, it is the only theatre where you can find live performances in the lobby every weekend. The tickets for weekend evenings after 6p.m. in the Director Hall start at 14 dollars and a standard ticket costs 10.75 while the Center stage prices are 9.75.

극장 좌석이 앞 좌석과 거리가 2피트가 넘고 가죽으로 만들어졌으며 로비에서 매 주말 라이브 공연을 하는 곳은 세계에서 이 곳밖에 없다. 티켓 가격은 가죽 좌석이 있는 디렉터스 홀의 경우 주말 저녁(오후 6시 이후) 14달러, 주말 조조할인 10.75달러, 센터 스테이지 주말 저녁 가격은 9.75달러 등이다.

1. 특급 호텔을 연상시키는 2003년 개장한 The Bridge 극장 : LA's multiplex theatres include the Bridge and Hollywood(Arclight Hollywood), which is reminiscent of a luxury hotel built in 2003. 유명한 LA의 극장으로는 '더 브리지'(The Bridge)와 아클라이트 할리웃(Arclight Hollywood)이 있습니다.

2. 고급 스포츠 바에 버금가는 시설을 자랑하는 브리지의 12라운지

3. At the Arc light Cinema

 참고 사이트

• 미국영화관 AMC
http://www.amcentertainment.com/

• I tune apple Trailer
http://trailers.apple.com/

Chapter 12

Throwing a **S**urprise **B**irthday **P**arty for **M**ike

Topic	Having a Surprise Birthday Party for Mike
Summary	Yuna decided to throw a surprise birthday party for Mike.

주제	마이크를 위한 깜짝 생일 파티
줄거리	유나는 마이크를 위해 깜짝 생일 파티를 열기로 결심했다.

Pre-check Quiz ✳

Q. 다음 중 의미 설명이 틀린 것을 고르시오.

   a. surprise – 놀래다

   b. hold a birthday cake – 생일 케이크를 들다

   c. be touched – 때리다

   d. icing – 당의, 아이싱

Dialogue ✳

Mike   Hey, what's going on here?

Yuna   Surprise! Happy Birthday Mike!

Mike   You scared me to death.

(Holding a lit birthday cake)

Yuna   Now make a wish and blow out the candles.

(After blowing out the candles, Yuna puts icing on Mike's nose.)

Mike   So now what? Is this all you've prepared?

Yuna   You know it is not the gift that counts, it's what's inside.

Mike   No, I was just kidding. I am really touched.

마이크   이봐, 무슨 일이 일어나고 있는 거야?

유나   깜짝 놀랐지! 마이크, 생일 축하해!

마이크   간 떨어질 뻔했잖아.

(촛불이 켜진 생일 케이크를 들고)

유나   소원을 빌고 촛불을 꺼.

(촛불을 끈 후 유나는 마이크의 코에 아이싱을 묻힌다.)

마이크   그래서 다음은 뭐야? 네가 준비한 게 이게 다야?

유나   선물보단 선물에 든 마음을 보라고.

마이크   알아. 농담이야. 정말 감동했어.

Comprehension Questions

1. **Why does Mike say "You scared me to death."?**

   a. He's going to die.

   b. He was very surprised.

   c. He thought Yuna was dead.

   HINT Surprise! Happy Birthday Mike!

2. **Why does Yuna say, "It's not the gift that counts."?**

   a. Because Mike hates parties.

   b. Because she couldn't find the proper amount of candles.

   c. Because Mike seemed disappointed.

   HINT You know it is not the gift that counts, it's what's inside.

02 **V**ocabulary

1. surprise : 놀라다

   (used to describe when something unexpected happens; can also be used to describe shock)

2. be touched : 감동받다

   (=to experience feelings of deep sentimental value, sadness or happiness)

3. hold a lit birthday cake : 생일 케이크를 들다

   light the candles　　　　: 촛불을 켜다

   light up a cigarette　　　: 담배에 불을 붙이다

4. icing : 아이싱/당의

   (=the sweet creamy topping found on cakes, sweet breads or pastries)

1. **You scared me to death.** 간 떨어질 뻔했다.

표현설명

used to express unexpected shock or surprise

상황

Mike : Hey, what's going on here? (이봐, 무슨 일이 일어나고 있는 거야?)

Yuna : Surprise! Happy Birthday Mike! (깜짝 놀랐지! 마이크, 생일 축하해!)

Mike : You scared me to death. (간 떨어질 뻔했잖아.)

응용문제

Anna is sitting in the bookstore, quietly reading. Her friend Tammy, excited that her boyfriend has just asked her to marry him, comes in behind her.

(Anna는 서점에 앉아 조용히 책을 읽고 있다. 최근에 남자 친구한테 청혼을 받아 신나있는 그녀의 친구, Tammy가 뒤에서 온다.)

Tammy : Boo! Guess what? (야! 너 그거 알아?)

Anna : (She is surprised, jumps a little in her seat.)

Oh my god, Tammy, _____!

((놀라 의자에서 살짝 들썩이며) 어머나, Tammy, 나 간 떨어질 뻔했다.)

2. **Now make a wish and blow out the candles.** 이제 소원을 빌고 촛불을 꺼라.

표현설명

What a person says after singing the birthday song and just before the cake cutting/eating.

상황

(Holding a lit birthday cake) (촛불이 켜진 생일 케이크를 들고)

Yuna : Now make a wish and blow out the candles. (소원을 빌고 촛불을 꺼.)

Family and friends : (singing) Happy Birthday to you!
((노래 부르며) 생일 축하합니다!)

Mother : Okay Ashton! _____.
(자 에쉬톤! 소원을 빌고 촛불을 끄렴.)

Ashton : (closes his eyes, pauses, and then blows hard at the candles)
(눈을 감고 잠시 있다가 힘껏 촛불을 끈다.)

Family and friends : (cheering) Hooray!!! (clapping)
(환호하며) 야호! (박수를 친다.)

3. **It's the thought that counts.** 성의가 중요하죠.

What is said at times when you receive a disappointing gift, but you still want to express your appreciation.

Mike : So now what? Is this all you've prepared?
(그래서 다음은 뭐야? 네가 준비한 거 이게 다야?)

Yuna : You know it is not the gift that counts, it's what's inside.
(선물보단 선물에 든 마음을 보라고.)

Mike : No, I was just kidding. I am really touched.
(알아. 농담이야. 정말 감동했어.)

Carla : Hi Melissa, what did you and Todd do for your birthday this year?
(안녕 말리사, 올해 너 생일 때 너랑 토드랑 뭐했니?)

Melissa : Well, Todd took me to a baseball game.
(음, 토드가 날 야구 경기에 데리고 갔어.)

Carla : Oh no! You don't even like baseball!
(어머! 너 야구 싫어하잖아.)

Melissa : I know, but _____, right?
(그렇지만 마음이 중요한 거니까, 그렇지?)

04 Pattern Practice

1. Basic

Now ~ and ~ . (이제 ~을 하고 ~을 해라.)

1 이제 눈을 감고 소원을 빌어라.

Now _____.

2 이제 음악을 듣고 음악에 춤을 춰라.

Now _____.

3 이제 준비하시고, 출발.

Now _____.

2. One Step Further

This is all ~. (이것이 ~한 전부다.)

1 이것이 제일 중요한 거다.

This is all _____.

2 이게 너에게 원하는 전부다.

This is all _____.

3 이것이 너에게 줄 수 있는 전부다.

This is all _____.

1. I was so _____ to see that this answer was wrong.

   a. surprise　　　　　　　　b. shocking

   c. surprising　　　　　　　d. shocked

   HINT 사람이 직접 감정을 받을 땐 빈칸의 단어가 수동형이어야 한다. (BE+ PP)

2. This movie is very _____. I especially like the part when Darcy meets Helen.

   a. moved　　　　　　　　　b. touch

   c. touching　　　　　　　　d. thrilled

   HINT 어떠한 사물이나 사람 등이 감정을 느끼게 하는 주체가 될 때 현재분사로 써야 한다.

3. Please _____ this candle carefully.

   a. pulls　　　　　　　　　　b. touchs

   c. grabbing　　　　　　　　d. hold

   HINT 주어가 없는 명령문 찾기

06 **A**uto-**M**emorization

1. surprise : 놀랐지?/놀라다
   Surprise! Happy Birthday Mike!

2. be touched : 감동 받다
   I am really touched.

3. hold/light : 들다/불을 붙이다
   Hold a lit birthday cake.

4. icing : 아이싱
   Yuna puts icing on Mike's nose.

1. 연상 퀴즈

1 Tammy : Boo! Guess what?
(야! 그거 알아?)

Anna : Oh my god, _____.
(아 깜짝이야. 간 떨어질 뻔했잖아.)

2 Jack : Wow, a birthday cake!
(우와, 생일 케이크네!)

Jill   : Yes, _____.
(응, 이제 소원을 빌고 촛불 꺼.)

2. Tapping

- Surprise! : 깜짝 놀랐지?
- I am touched. : 나 감동했어.

3. Pattern Practice

이제 눈을 감고 소원을 빌어라.

Now close your eyes and (make a wish).

💬 과제 작문 연습

Key phrase를 가지고 두 사람이 대화를 하는 상황을 만들어 보세요.

Key phrase : **It's the thought that counts.**

* 생일 케이크

History of Birthday Cake can be traced back to the ancient Greeks who made round or moon shaped honey cakes or bread and took it to the temple of Artemis – the Goddess of Moon. Nowadays people place candles on Birthday cakes. It is believed that blowing out all candles in one breath means the wish will come true. Some also speak out the name of the birthday boy/girl before slicing of the cake to bring good luck.

생일 케이크의 유래는 고대 그리스로 거슬러 올라가는데, 그 당시 사람들은 달의 여신인 아르테미스의 신전에 동그란 모양의 꿀 케익 혹은 빵을 바쳤다. 현대에 와선 생일 당사자가 케이크에 촛불을 꽂고 촛불을 불기 전에 마음 속으로 소망을 빈다. 한 번에 촛불을 다 끄는 것은 그 소망이 이루어진다는 뜻이며 그 다음 해 행운이 가득하다는 의미를 지닌다. 몇몇 다른 사람들은 생일 케이크를 자르기 전 생일인 사람에게 행운을 주기 위해 그 사람의 이름을 크게 부르기도 한다.

In medieval times, England people used to place symbolic objects like coins, rings and thimbles in the batter of the cake. If the cake fell while baking it was considered to be a bad omen and bad luck for the person in the coming year.

중세 시대엔 영국 사람들은 케이크 빵 안에 동전, 반지 혹은 골무 등을 넣기도 하였다. 만약 케이크가 구워지는 중 떨어졌다면 이는 불길한 징조임을 뜻하며 그 다음 해 불운이 온다고 믿었다.

 참고 사이트

* Origins of Birthday Cakes
http://www.tokenz.com/history-of-birthday-cake.html

* Words for Birthday Wishes
http://www.yourdictionary.com/library/grammar/style-and-usage/words-for-birthday-wishes.html

Chapter 13

Review

Dialogue ✱

Yuna Hi, I can't withdraw money from the ATM with this card. What's wrong?

Teller Oh, I see. This is a domestic card. It cannot be used overseas.

Yuna Then do I need to open an account here?

Teller Yes. It's very simple. Just fill out this form and show me two forms of ID.

Yuna I have a passport and a student ID.

Teller That's the ticket.

Comprehension Questions

1. Why can't Yuna withdraw money from the bank?

   a. The ATM machine is out of order.

   b. The bank is closed.

   c. The card has been blocked.

   d. Domestic cards cannot be used overseas.

   HINT This is a domestic card. It cannot be used overseas.

2. What should Yuna do to withdraw money from the bank?

   a. Call the domestic bank.

   b. Open a new account with the overseas bank.

   c. Use the online banking system.

   d. Change her password.

   HINT Then do I need to open an account here? – Yes.

Chapter 09

🎧 Dialogue ✳

Yuna	Wow, that store is having a clearance sale. I need new shoes.
Mike	Me too. I could use a new pair of slippers.

(In the shoe store)

Yuna	Hi, I'm in the market for a practical pair of pumps. My size is 240.
Clerk	Pardon me, but do you know the American size?
Yuna	Ah! Sorry, I think it is size 7.
Clerk	Here you are. They are 30% off today, so they are $79. They are the hottest item.
Yuna	What a steal! I will take them.

Comprehension Questions

1. **What type of shoes is Mike looking for?**

   a. a pair of practical pumps   b. a pair of boots

   c. a pair of sneakers   d. a pair of slippers

   HINT I could use a new pair of slippers.

2. **What does the clerk mean when she says 'hottest item'?**

   a. Shoes that are out of stock

   b. The best-selling shoes

   c. The most expensive shoes

   d. Shoes that are worn in the summer

   HINT Here you are. They are 30% off today, so they are $79. They are the hottest item.

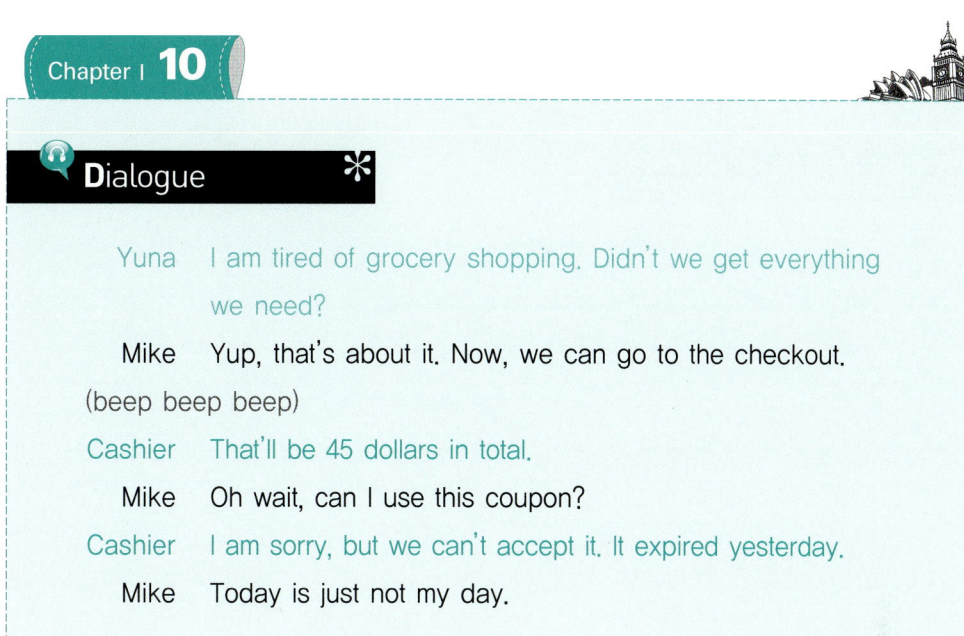

Dialogue ✳

Yuna I am tired of grocery shopping. Didn't we get everything we need?

Mike Yup, that's about it. Now, we can go to the checkout.

(beep beep beep)

Cashier That'll be 45 dollars in total.

Mike Oh wait, can I use this coupon?

Cashier I am sorry, but we can't accept it. It expired yesterday.

Mike Today is just not my day.

Comprehension Questions

1. Which item is not considered something you purchase while 'grocery shopping'?

   a. milk   b. bread

   c. meat   d. pencil

   HINT Grocery shopping means shopping for food items.

2. What does Mike mean when he says 'Today is just not my day.'?

   a. He is very busy today.

   b. Today is not his birthday.

   c. Things are not going well for him today.

   d. Today is his lucky day.

   HINT I am sorry, but we can't accept it. It expired yesterday.

Chapter 11

Dialogue ✳

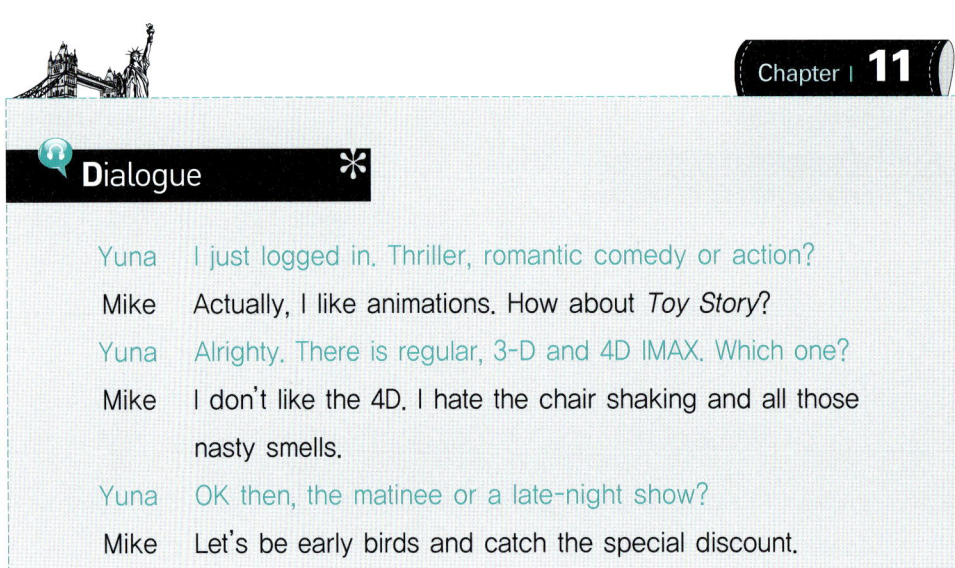

Yuna   I just logged in. Thriller, romantic comedy or action?

Mike   Actually, I like animations. How about *Toy Story*?

Yuna   Alrighty. There is regular, 3-D and 4D IMAX. Which one?

Mike   I don't like the 4D. I hate the chair shaking and all those nasty smells.

Yuna   OK then, the matinee or a late-night show?

Mike   Let's be early birds and catch the special discount.

Comprehension Questions

1. What type of movie theater doesn't Mike like?

   a. Regular screening

   b. 3D screening

   c. 4D screening

   d. IMAX screening

   HINT   I don't like the 4D. I hate the chair shaking and all those nasty smells.

2. Why does Mike want to watch the matinee?

   a. The movie he wants to watch only plays in the morning.

   b. There is a special discount in the daytime.

   c. He has other plans at night.

   d. He does not like to stay out at night.

   HINT   Let's be early birds and catch the special discount.

🎧 **D**ialogue ✳

Mike   Hey what's going on here?

Yuna   Surprise! Happy Birthday Mike!

Mike   You scared me to death.

(Holding a lit birthday cake)

Yuna   Now make a wish and blow out the candles.

(After blowing out the candles, Yuna puts icing on Mike's nose.)

Mike   So now what? Is this all you've prepared?

Yuna   You know it is not the gift that's important. It's the thought that counts.

Mike   No, I was just kidding. I am really touched.

Comprehension Questions

1. **What type of party is this?**

   a. a year-end party

   b. a surprise birthday party

   c. a farewell party

   d. an impromptu gathering

   HINT Surprise! Happy Birthday Mike!

2. **What does Yuna find most important?**

   a. expensive gifts   b. birthday cakes

   c. one's innermost thoughts   d. the tradition

   HINT You know it is not the gift that's important. It's the thought that counts.

1. Foreigners can also open an account _____ an overseas bank.

   a. on

   b. about

   c. to

   d. with

   HINT '~과'의 의미를 가지고 있는 전치사구 찾기

2. Making a tuna sandwich is very _____.

   a. easily

   b. simple

   c. bored

   d. briefly

   HINT 〈명사+be 동사+형용사〉 구조 찾기

3. Taking yoga classes may be just the _____ for losing weight.

   a. lock

   b. form

   c. ticket

   d. paper

   HINT '바로 그거면 됩니다/딱이다'라는 관용어구 표현 찾기

4. I am _____ school to meet my professor.

   a. out

   b. into

   c. at

   d. between

   HINT '~에 오다'라는 장소를 표현할 때 쓰이는 전치사 찾기

5. What a _____! It costs only ten dollars.

    a. low

    b. steal

    c. cheap

    d. nothing

    HINT "너무 싸다"라는 관용어구 표현 찾기

6. This pink lipstick is _____ than the orange one.

    a. hottest

    b. hot

    c. more popular

    d. warm

    HINT 원급, 비교급과 최상급을 파악하기. 비교급 뒤에 than이 따라온다.

7. I am sorry, but I cannot _____ your offer.

    a. accepted

    b. except

    c. accept

    d. exacting

    HINT 발음과 스펠링이 비슷한 단어들 중에서 '받아들이다/허용하다'의 의미를 갖는 단어

8. The _____ date for this coupon was yesterday.

    a. expiring

    b. expiratory

    c. expiration

    d. expire

    HINT '만료일'이라는 표현. expiratory는 '숨 쉬는'이라는 의미

9. I am tired _____ listening to your lies.

    a. in

    b. about

    c. of

    d. out

    HINT tired of(싫증나다/지긋지긋하다/지겹다)라는 의미의 표현. tired out : 녹초가 되었다

10. Don't forget to _____ out when you are done with your email.

    a. log

    b. tree

    c. blow

    d. get

    HINT '계정 종료'의 영어 표현. log는 통나무의 뜻도 있다. blow out은 '불어서 불을 끄다'는 의미

11. I prefer _____ movies to horror movies.

    a. act

    b. active

    c. activate

    d. action

    HINT act라는 단어의 어원에서 나오는 다른 의미의 단어. activate : 활성화시키다, active : 활동적인

12. Don't you know that the early _____ gets the worm?

    a. fish

    b. cat

    c. bird

    d. man

    HINT '아침형 사람'이라는 표현

13. I hate the chair shaking and water _____ in 4D movie theaters.

   a. spray

   b. sprayed

   c. spraying

   d. sprays

> HINT hate the chair shaking(동사+목적어+ing)의 형태에서 and로 병렬 구조를 취해야 한다.

14. The streetlight is _____ dimly.

   a. light

   b. lit

   c. lighting

   d. lightness

> HINT be동사+pp(light-lit-lit) / light : 불을 켜다

15. I thought I lost you. You scared me _____ death!

   a. for

   b. to

   c. as

   d. like

> HINT '매우 놀라다'라는 뜻의 덩어리 표현

16. _____ overseas experience is recommended for language learners.

   a. Many

   b. A few

   c. A lots

   d. Much

> HINT experience(경험)는 불가산 명사

17. He wants to study _____ English rather than English literature.

    a. use

    b. skill

    c. practical

    d. practice

    HINT   '실용적인'이란 의미를 띄는 단어로 명사인 'English'를 꾸미는 형용사 필요

18. I need a new pair of _____.

    a. slipper

    b. sandal

    c. jean

    d. scissors

    HINT   a pair는 한 쌍이기 때문에 항상 짝이 있는 단어가 와야 함. (ex) jeans, shoes, glasses

19. I've got 4 quarters and 5 dimes now. In total, I _____ $1.50.

    a. has

    b. had

    c. having

    d. have

    HINT   대명사 'I'에 맞는 시제 동사 찾기

20. What a _____ movie! I wasted my time and money.

    a. boring

    b. awful

    c. delicious

    d. bored

    HINT   어떠한 사물이나 사람 등이 감정을 느끼게 하는 주체가 될 때 현재분사로 써야 한다.

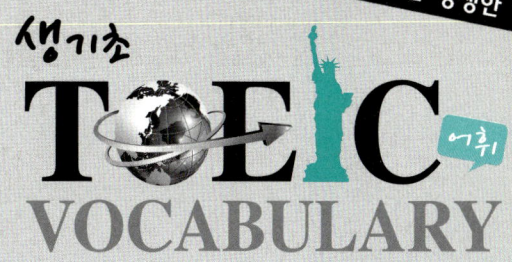

Chapter 01　Preparing to Go Abroad

* **Pre-check Quiz** : a

01. Comprehension Questions

1. d

[해설] Mr. Smith가 "You are BOTH"라고 했으며 여기서 Both는 '둘 다'라는 의미로 유나와 마이크를 가리키는 말이다.

2. c

[해설] 다른말로 바꾸어 표현하는(paraphrases) 능력이 필요하다.

working visa → a visa that permits employment(고용이 가능한 비자), 여권, 비자 그리고 운전면허증이 필요하다고 했으므로 국제신용카드는 해당이 안 됨.

03. Expressions

1. I got the spot
2. Speak of the devil

04. Pattern Practice

1. **1** take her out tonight
   2 throw/have a party
   3 get a hairdo

2. **1** buy to please her
   2 wear for the party
   3 drink at the fancy restaurant

05. TOEIC 실전 문제 풀이

1. b

[해석] 우선 레프팅을 즐기기 위해선 구명 조끼를 입어야 한다.

[해설] 문장 속 역할은 부사(=firstly, at first, first of all) → a,c,d는 다 명사 형태로 품사적으로 제외 가능하다. a는 도전자, c는 회사 임원, d는 직원이므로 '우선'이라는 의미의 first of all이 맞음. 따라서 정답은 b이다. 참고로 For가 붙지 않은 그냥 명사형의 starters는 '일을 처음 시작하는 사람, 애송이'라는 뜻이다.

2. a

[해석] 이 전자 파일은 다른 컴퓨터로 옮겨져야 한다.

[해설] 품사적으로 be transferred 형태는 be동사 다음에 오는 과거분사의 결합으로 수동의 의미를 지닌다. b는 원형동사로 제외, a,c,d가 가능하다.(proofread는 과거분사도 철자가 동일) 문맥의 의미상 c, d를 선택하면 "이 전자 문서는 다른 컴퓨터로 교정/수정되어야 한다"가 되므로 어색하다. move 이동하다 / delete 삭제하다 / proofread 교정하다 / change 변경하다

3. d

[해석] 신청서를 다 작성하고 이력서와 함께 준비해두세요.

[해설] 동사인 complete(완료) 다음에 관사가 나오므로 그 다음에 명사가 나와야 한다. 따라서, 명사형인 d만 가능하다. apply 신청하다, 적용하다 / applicable 적용할 수 있는

07. Wrap Up

1. ❶ I got the spot   ❷ Speak of the devil

Chapter 02   Checking In for the Flight

* **Pre-check Quiz** : c

01. Comprehension Questions

1. c

[해설] 토익에서 단수와 복수 구분은 중요하다. 질문에서 which items 즉, 복수를 묻고 있으므로 a, d는 제외하고 b, c가 가능성이 있는데 대화에서 제시된 것은 여권과 티켓이다.

2. c

[해설] baggage allowance(수하물 허용량)는 check in을 할 때 허용되는 짐의 무게를 말하므로 얼마나 많은 백을 직접 손에 들고 비행기에 탈수 있는가를 의미한다.

03. Expressions

1 How many freaking bags are you checking in today

2 it seems, you weigh a ton

04. Pattern Practice

1. ❶ Put (your cell phone) on the table
   ❷ your sunglasses
   ❸ your earrings

2. ❶ put your cell phone on the table
   ❷ put on your sunglasses
   ❸ put on your hat

05. TOEIC 실전 문제 풀이

1. a

   [해석] 이 가방은 매우 무겁다.

   [해설] weighs a ton은 단어 그대로 1톤 무게라는 의미로 쓰일 수도 있고 비유적으로 굉장히 무겁다는 의미로 쓰일 수도 있다. 문맥을 보고 결정해야 하는데 주어가 baggage(짐)이므로 정답은 a가 된다. c는 '복잡하다', d는 '수하물이 부쳐지면 안 된다'는 뜻이다.

2. d

   [해석] 일인당 수화물 허용량은 20킬로 미만이다.

   [해설] 동사가 is이므로 b, c는 복수 주어로 답이 될 수 없고 a, d만 가능하다. a는 '손으로 들고 가는 가방', d는 '허용할 수 있는 짐 무게'라는 뜻이므로 정답은 d가 된다. 참고로 b는 '무게가 초과된 가방', c는 '여행 가방'이라는 뜻이다.

3. a

   [해석] 체크인 카운터에 티켓을 올려주세요.

   [해설] 주어가 없이 시작하는 명령문이다. 동사원형이 아닌 b, c는 제외되고 a, d 중 답이 있는데 a는 '체크인 카운터에 티켓을 올려주세요.'의 의미를 갖고 있고 d는 '체크인 카운터에 티켓의 무게를 재어 주세요.'라는 의미이다. 따라서 답은 a이다.

07. Wrap Up

1. ❶ check in   ❷ weighs a ton

Chapter 03 Immigration Interview

✳ Pre-check Quiz : e

01. Comprehension Questions

1. c

   [해설] 토익에서 의문문의 경우 처음에 나오는 의문사에 집중해야 하는데 where가 장소이므로 답으로 c,d만 가능하다. 질문이 how long이었으면 a, with whom이었으면 b가 답이 된다.

2. d

   [해설] 캘리포니아 대학에 어학 연수하러 왔으므로 d가 정답이다. b가 혼돈될 수 있는데 캘리포니아를 연구하러 온 것이 아니므로 정답이 될 수 없다.

03. Expressions

1. ❶ What's the purpose of your visit?　❷ What brings you here?
2. top notch
3. Where will you stay
4. Enjoy the California sunshine

04. Pattern Practice

1. ❶ your smart-phone
   ❷ your exam note
   ❸ your ID

2. ❶ the smart-phone, but be careful with it
   ❷ the exam note, but don't pass it around
   ❸ my ID/I'm 23

05. TOEIC 실전 문제 풀이

1. d

   [해석] 이 발표의 주요 목적은 우리 회사를 소개하기 위해서이다.

   [해설] 동사인 a, b는 제외된다. c, d는 명사이나 '의도, 목적'의 뜻과 부합하는 d가 정답이다. c는 '발표의 장점'이라는 의미가 되므로 적절하지 않다.

2. b

   [해석] 삼성전자는 역사와 규모로 볼 때 명문 기업이다.

[해설] a. history(역사)와 d. indifference(무관심)는 명사이므로 제외. c. challenging은 '어려운'이라는 뜻으로 문맥상 의미가 다르다. 결국 '명문'의 뜻과 부합하는 b가 정답이다.

3. a

[해석] 우리 당분간 서로 보지 말자.

[해설] for good은 forever라는 뜻이지만 여기서는 관사가 붙었기 때문에 의미가 사라진다. on purpose의 뜻은 '의도적으로, 일부러'라는 뜻이 있지만 for라는 전치사가 이미 있기 때문에 전치사가 중복된다. 또한, for sale이란 '판매 중'이라는 굳은 표현이지만 이 문맥에서는 맞지 않다.

07. Wrap Up

1. ❶ what brings you　　　　　　　　❷ Youth Hostel

| Chapter 04 | Asking for Directions |

✻ Pre-check Quiz : d

01. Comprehension Questions

1. c

[해설] final destination은 '목적지'를 의미한다.

2. d

[해설] 기름을 채우려고 주유소에 들어온 건 아니라고 하면서 길을 묻는다.

03. Expressions

1. We need to ask someone for directions

2. How do I get to the post office

3. ❶ you can't miss it　　　　　　❷ You can't miss it

04. Pattern Practice

1. ❶ Disneyland　　　　　　　2. ❶ Disneyland by bus

　❷ Korea/Korean town　　　　　❷ Korea Town by metro

❸ Santa Monica Beach   ❸ Santa Monica Beach on foot

❹ Hollywood   ❹ Hollywood by car

05. TOEIC 실전 문제 풀이

1. b

[해석] 이 잔을 오렌지 주스로 채워주세요.

[해설] Phrasal Verb(구절 동사)의 중요성!

2. c

[해석] 이 단지에서 왼쪽으로 가면 사무실이 있는 건물이 보이실 겁니다.

[해설] a는 왼쪽을 건너뛰다, b는 왼쪽으로 가로지르다, d는 왼쪽으로 떠나다. '돌다'라는 의미인 c가 정답이다.

3. a

[해석] 그를 따라가자. 그는 길을 알아.

[해설] follow는 타동사로써 목적어를 바로 취할 수 있다.

[ex] Discuss the matter.(o) Discuss with the matter.(x)

07. Wrap Up

1. ❶ hang a left   ❷ regular or diesel

Chapter 05 Shopping at the Flea Market

✳ Pre-check Quiz : b

01. Comprehension Questions

1. a

[해설] 마음대로 추측은 금지다. mint condition(새 것 같은)이라는 표현에 따라 상상하여 two weeks라고 하면 안 된다. 답은 지문에 써있는 것과 같이 2년이다.

2. c

[해설] delivery service를 포함하지 않는 조건으로 제시한 마지막 offer는 85달러이다.

bucks＝dollars

03. Expressions

1. **1** mint condition   **2** mint condition
2. **1** what's your asking price   **2** What's your asking price
3. **1** bleed us dry   **2** bleeding us dry
4. **1** no delivery service   **2** no delivery service

04. Pattern Practice

1. **1** lose weight
   2 ask her out / buy her heart
   3 get straight A's

2. **1** buy her heart
   2 break her heart
   3 get a good grade

05. TOEIC 실전 문제 풀이

1. c

[해석] 만약 당신이 제시하는 마지막 가격이 5달러라면 전 이 필통을 사지 않겠습니다.

[해설] offer가 명사이므로 앞에는 형용사가 와야 한다. b. finalize와 d. reasonably는 각각 동사와 부사이므로 답에서 제외된다. a. good은 의미상 답이 될 수 없고 best offer라면 답이 될 수 있다. 따라서 '최종 가격'이라는 의미의 c가 정답이다.

2. c

[해석] 브라운 씨는 회의에서 연설을 할 예정이다.

[해설] a는 '출산하다', b는 '보내다', d는 '수송하다'이므로 문맥상 c가 정답이다.

3. a

[해석] 어차피 싸니까 이 쿠션을 사겠어요.

[해설] 뜻을 알고 있어야 해당하는 접속사를 고를 수 있다. a. since : because, b. because of : ~ 때문에 (뒤에 명사가 와야 한다 [ex] because of the low price), c. however : 그러나, 하지만 (앞 내용과 상반되는 내용이 와야 한다.), d. therefore : 그렇기 때문에 (원인과 결과가 뒤바뀜 → It's a steal therefore I will buy this cushion.) 따라서 답은 a. since다.

07. Wrap Up

1. **1** delivery service   **2** Deal

Chapter 06　Go Sightseeing

✳ Pre-check Quiz : a

01. Comprehension Questions

1. c

[해설] per person은 each의 의미이다. 입장료가 각각 129달러고 두 명의 입장료를 지불해야 하므로 $258가 정답이다.

2. c

[해설] 마이크의 발이 아프기 때문이다. be동사 다음에 들어갈 수 있는 진행형이 적절하다. a,b는 동사원형이어서 안되고 d. pain은 명사이므로 안된다. 따라서 c가 정답이다. hurt는 타동사로 '아프게 하다'라는 의미이다.

03. Expressions

1. admission tickets are kind of pricey
2. How much is admission
3. my feet are killing me

04. Pattern Practice

1. ❶ The homework is killing me.

　❷ This high heel is killing me.

　❸ This project presentation is killing me.

2. ❶ This course is a killer content.

　❷ The singer Rain has a six pack on his body. He is such a killer.

　❸ The girl I have a crush on has a killer voice.

05. TOEIC 실전문제 풀이

1. c

[해석] 이 철 지난 겉옷은 꽤 비싼 반면 신상품은 합리적인 가격이다.

[해설] a. because of는 전치사구로 '~때문에'라는 뜻이다. b. due to도 마찬가지로 '~때문에'라는 의

✳ Answer

미로 because of와 마찬가지로 뒤에 명사가 와야 한다. [ex] due to high demand (수요가 많아서) 마지막으로, d의 after all은 부사로 '결국에는'이라는 뜻이다.

2. a

[해석] 네가 공부하는 것을 좋아하는 이상 후회는 없을 것이다.

[해설] a를 제외한 나머지는 전치사구로 뒤에 '주어+동사'가 올 수 없고 명사가 와야 한다.

3. c

[해석] 이 곳의 여우들이 아주 사납다는 사실을 알고 있어야 해.

[해설] be aware of=recognize : 인식하다 / be fond of : 좋아하다

　　　 d. should 다음에는 동사원형이 와야 하므로 are aware는 적절하지 않다.

07. Wrap Up

1. **1** How much is admission?　　　　**2** My feet are killing me.

Chapter 07　Review

01. Comprehension Questions

1. c

[해설] Mr. Smith가 "You are BOTH"라고 했으니 즉, 유나와 마이크 둘 다 해외 지사로 발령된다는 뜻이다. 따라서 해외 지사로 발령되지 않은 사람은 Mr. Smith이다.

2. a

[해설] 마이크의 발령 소식은 엿들었지만 자신의 발령 소식은 Mr. Smith에게 직접 들었다.

02. Comprehension Questions

1. b

[해설] check for dangerous item : 위험한 물건을 조사하다

2. d

[해설] a의 oversized는 사이즈를 말하고 있지만 대화에서는 무게에 대해 말하고 있다.

03. Comprehension Questions

1. a

[해설] study : 공부하다 / work : 일하다 / conference : 회의

2. c

[해설] 우와. 거기 정말 최고의 학교잖아.

04. Comprehension Questions

1. a

[해설] 남자는 길을 묻기 위해 gas station을 가르키고 있다.

2. d

[해설] turn left = hang left : 왼쪽으로 돌다

05. Comprehension Questions

1. b

[해설] mint condition : 상태가 양호하다

2. b

[해설] $100에서 $85로 할인해줬다.

06. Comprehension Questions

1. b

[해설] worth it : 가치가 있다

2. a

[해설] 마이크는 발이 아파서 앉아야겠다고 말한다.

✱ TOEIC 실전 문제 풀이

1. b

[해석] 수영하기 전에 우선 준비 운동을 해야 한다.

2. a

[해석] 그가 본사로 옮겨질 거라고 들었다.

3. a

[해석] 한국을 떠나기 전에 국제 운전 면허증을 취득하는 것이 좋다.

4. d

[해석] 신청서는 저 카운터에 있습니다.

5. c

[해석] 가방을 몇 개 부치실 건가요?

6. d

[해석] 이 가방들은 수하물 허용량을 초과했습니다. 20킬로 미만이어야 합니다.

7. b

[해석] 이 병을 선반에 놔주세요.

8. d

[해석] 이 프로모션의 가장 중요한 목적은 판매를 증대시키는 것이다.

9. b

[해석] 하버드 대학은 미국 최고의 학교 중 하나이다.

10. a

[해석] 당분간 내 가방 좀 봐줘.

11. a

[해석] 그는 오늘 아침 방을 풍선으로 가득 채웠다.

12. c

[해석] 직진하다 보면 오른쪽으로 가라는 신호가 보일 거야.

13. d

[해석] 나는 오바마 대통령의 트위터를 따르고 있다.

14. c

[해석] 이 책상의 마지막이자 최고 가격을 말해주세요.

15. b

[해석] 반기문 사무총장은 지난 주 UN 회의에서 연설을 했다.

16. a

   [해석] 가격이 아주 싸니까 이것으로 10켤레 주세요.

17. c

   [해석] 그들은 보수주의 쪽에 근접한 반면 우리는 진보주의 쪽에 있다.

18. a

   [해석] 날씨가 좋은 이상 우리는 캠핑을 하러 갈 것이다.

19. b

   [해석] 이 드레스는 너무 비싸다. 이것을 살 여유가 안 된다.

20. d

   [해석] 작은 피자는 나에게 충분하지 않다.

Chapter 08   Opening a Bank Account

＊ Pre-check Quiz : a

01. Comprehension Questions

   1. b

   [해설] 유나는 한국에서 썼던 카드를 미국 ATM 기기에서 사용하려고 해서 인출이 안 된 것이다.
   Yuna의 입장에서 그 카드는 [domestic → 국내 → 한국] 카드를 뜻한다.

   2. a

   [해설] 2가지 형태의 ID를 요구했으므로 b. passport는 단수로 제외시킨다. 유나가 제시한 두 가지
   신분증은 여권과 학생증이다.(Passport and Student ID)

03. Expressions

   1. I cannot withdraw money from the ATM
   2. I need to open a new account
   3. 1 just the ticket

       2 that's just the ticket

04. Pattern Practice

1. **1** I filled out my resume.

   2 I filed out job application for Samsung Electronics Corporation.

   3 Fill out the college application, and I'll print it out for you.

2. **1** Why don't you fill out the survey sheet?

   2 Why don't you fill out the wedding registration?

   3 Why don't you fill out this form?

05. TOEIC 실전 문제 풀이

1. b

   [해석] 저기 있는 현금인출기에서 돈을 지급받을 수 있습니다.

   [해설] ATM은 현금인출기이다. 가장 비슷한 뜻을 가지고 있는 단어가 b. cash machine이고 c. secured loan은 '담보 대출', d. truck of money는 '돈 트럭'이라는 뜻이기 때문에 답이 될 수 없다.

2. a

   [해석] 당신에게 술을 팔려면 신분증을 확인해야 합니다.

   [해설] ID는 신분증으로 a. identification의 약자입니다. ideal card에서 ideal은 '이상적인'이라는 뜻으로 d는 오답이다. student number는 학번을 뜻하므로 student card number와 헷갈리면 안된다.

3. d

   [해석] 이 아래의 서식을 작성해 주시겠습니까?

   [해설] fill out은 두 단어지만 숙어로써 '작성하다'라는 뜻을 가지고 있다. filled with는 '무엇으로 가득 채워진'이라는 뜻이며 수동태이므로 목적어가 있는 능동태 문장과 어울리지 않는다.

07. Wrap Up

1. **1** domestic card   **2** ID

Chapter 09　Buying Shoes

＊ Pre-check Quiz : c

01. Comprehension Questions

1. c

[해설] 유나의 미국식 발 사이즈는 7이니 한국식으로 240mm이다. 79는 신발의 가격이다.

2. d

[해설] I'll take them에서 them은 신발을 뜻하고 take는 '가져가다'의 의미이므로 신발을 집으로 가져간다는 것이니 '이 신발을 산다'라는 뜻이다. What a steal이 앞에 있어서 혹시 신발을 훔치거나 take를 '가져가다'로 생각할 수 있지만 쇼핑 상황에서는 take는 purchase, buy의 의미이다.

03. Expressions

1. I could use a new pair of slippers
2. I'm in the market for a practical pair of pumps

04. Pattern Practice

1. ① this university / study English

　② this project / learn Professor Kim's leadership

　③ this building / meet Mr. Brown

2. ① Are you here to buy shoes?

　② Are you here to get a free gift?

　③ Are you here to give a lecture?

05. TOEIC 실전 문제 풀이

1. d

[해석] 우리는 벼룩시장에서 중고 물품을 살 수 있다.

[해설] a. 계절이 끝날 때 하는 세일 / b. garbage는 쓰레기 **garage sale은 개인적인 차원에서 소규모로 진행되는 중고 시장이고 Flea market = Swap meet은 상업적인 차원에서 정기적으로 열리는 대규모 중고 시장이다. Swap meet에서 swap이란 '맞바꾸다'이고 meet는 '만나다'라는 뜻이다.

2. c

[해석] 이 슬리퍼 한 켤레는 50% 세일합니다.

[해설] offline은 '오프라인의'라는 뜻으로 적절하지 않다. drop은 '떨어지다'라는 의미를 지니고 있지만 이는 '(사람이) 훌쩍 내리다, 뛰어내리다, (경첩·턱 등이) 덜컥 내려지다' 등의 상황에서만 표현될 수 있으며 '물건의 가격이 내려가다'라는 의미로는 쓰지 않는다. '깎다, 세일하다'라는 뜻인 off와 근접한 의미는 discounted밖에 없다.

3. a

[해석] 이 모자는 이번 시즌에 가장 잘 팔리는 물건 중에 하나입니다.

[해설] one of the를 붙이면 '최고의 ~중 하나이다'라는 뜻을 나타내는 최상급(~est) 표현이다. 최고이긴 하지만 유일한 것은 아니다. 이 모자는 이번 시즌에서 제일 잘 나가는 물건 '중' 하나이다. 즉, 잘 나가는 물건들이 여러 개 있는데 그 중에 이 모자가 있다는 뜻이므로 반드시 item 다음에 복수형 s를 붙여야 한다. 이는 여러 개의 아이템 '들'을 표시하기 위한 것이다.

07. Wrap Up

1. **1** practical   **2** 90% off

Chapter 10　Going to the Supermarket

✳ **Pre-check Quiz** : b

01. Comprehension Questions

1. c

[해설] 의문사 Why로 질문하고 있으므로 원인에 해당되는 이유를 찾아야 한다. 명사인 b가 정답이 되려면 Who didn't take the coupon?으로 물어야 한다. 정답은 대화에서와 같이 '만료되다'라는 의미의 expired=out of date=outdated가 들어가 있는 c이다.

2. b

[해설] c. After~는 시간에 대한 질문으로 When did they check out?에 대한 답이 될 수 있다. a는 check가 동사로 사용되었기 때문에 장소에 대한 답이 아니고 정답은 b이다. 계산을 하고 나가는 곳, 즉, 계산대(명사)는 checkout이라고 표현한다.

03. Expressions

1. we've got everything we need
2. We can go to the checkout
3. This coupon expired last week
4. today is just not my day

04. Pattern Practice

1. **1** can you turn off the TV **2** can you pay back the money I lent you

   3 can you give me some privacy

2. **1** I broke your cup **2** I missed your class

   3 I didn't do the assignment

05. TOEIC 실전 문제 풀이

1. a

   [해석] 토마토 3개, 양파 다섯 망… 총 15달러 되겠습니다.

   [해설] b는 틀린 영어 표현. c는 '할인'이라는 뜻이고, d는 '현찰로'라는 뜻이므로 '총합'이라는 의미를
   지닌 a가 정답이다. In total은 어떠한 것의 총 계수 혹은 합이라는 뜻으로 하나의 완전한 숙어이
   다. In cash도 숙어이지만 문맥에 어울리지 않는다.

2. b

   [해석] 첫 번째 계산대는 5개 물품 이하 구매 고객들만을 위한 곳입니다.

   [해설] 명사가 필요한 시점에서 a는 전치사구, c는 동사이므로 정답에 해당되지 않는다. d는 명사 형태이
   지만 '안내 데스크'라는 뜻이므로 문장의 의미상 맞지 않는다.

3. c

   [해석] 이 전자레인지의 보증기간은 만료되었습니다. 따라서 고객님은 이제부터 수리비를 내야 합니다.

   [해설] have+pp는 현재완료형으로써 has 다음에 과거분사가 나와야 한다. 따라서 a는 정답이 될 수 없
   으며 b는 '경험하다', d는 '갱신되다'라는 뜻으로 의미상 어울리지 않는다. c의 run out은 run을
   원형이라고 생각하여 제외시킬 수도 있지만 run의 3형태는 run－ran－run이므로 과거분사의 run
   이라고 생각하면 정답은 c이다.

07. Wrap Up

1. **1** grocery shopping **2** check out

*Answer

Chapter 11 Making Movie Reservations through the Internet

* **Pre-check Quiz** : c

01. Comprehension Questions

1. b

[해설] 마이크가 애니메이션을 좋아한다고 해서 토이 스토리를 골랐다. The Animation *Toy story* is neither a thriller nor a romantic comedy. (토이 스토리는 스릴러도 로맨틱 코미디도 아니다.)

2. a

[해설] 마이크는 이상한 냄새와 의자가 흔들리는 효과가 싫다고 했다. 영화 자체가 싫은 것보단 4D 영화의 특성상 나오는 효과가 싫은 것이다.

03. Expressions

1. matinee, late night show
2. IMAX in 4-D, regular version
3. Then be the early bird and catch that laptop

04. Pattern Practice

1. **1** a drink tonight
   2 picking up a girl tonight
   3 window shopping

2. **1** this draft beer
   2 the appetizer
   3 the ending

05. TOEIC 실전 문제 풀이

1. a

[해석] 네가 스릴러 장르 영화를 좋아하지 않는다는 건 알지만 오늘은 내 생일이잖아. 어서 보러 가자.

[해설] 접속사가 나온다는 전제 아래 a,b,c,d 전부 정답이다. 하지만 여기선 첫 문장과 둘째 문장의 내용이 상반되므로 역접 접속사를 찾아야 한다. so, and, therefore는 등위, 대등접속사(문법상 동등한 관계에 있는 word(낱말), phrase(구), clause(절)를 서로 연결시키는 역할을 한다), but은 반대, 대조를 나타내는 역접 접속사(앞의 말과 대립되거나 반대되는 말이 뒤따를 때 쓰는 접속사)이므로 정답은 a이다.

2. b

[해석] 너 혼자서 R-Rated 영화를 볼 생각은 하지 마! 넌 아직 15살이야.

[해설] a는 아동 영화, c는 부모님이 동반하는 13세 이상 관람가, d는 부모님의 지도 하에 관람이 가능한 영화(모두 15살이면 볼 수 있는 영화이다.) 하지만 R-rated는 준 성인용의 영화로써 19세 이상의 어른이 동반해야만 볼 수 있는 영화이다. 15살인 아이는 혼자 볼 수 없는 영화이니 정답은 b이다.

3. a

[해석] 샘은 부지런한 얼리 버드야. 그는 해야 할 일을 절대로 미루지 않아.

[해설] an 다음에는 모음으로 시작하는 단어가 와야 하므로 n과 s로 시작하는 b와 c는 정답이 될 수 없다. earnest는 형용사이므로 단독으로 문장을 끝낼 수 없다. 따라서 a의 early bird가 문맥상, 문법적으로 맞는 정답이다.

07. Wrap Up

1. **1** romantic comedy   **2** matinee

Lesson 12   Throwing a Surprise Birthday Party for Mike

✳ Pre-check Quiz : c

01. Comprehension Questions

1. b

[해설] 우리나라에도 "간 떨어질 뻔했다"라는 표현이 있듯이 영어에도 비슷한 표현이 있다. a는 실제로 마이크가 죽을 것이 아니기 때문에 오답이다.

2. c

[해설] 정답은 '마이크가 실망한 것처럼 보였기에'의 c이다. 주의할 점은 마이크가 진짜 실망해서 유나가 이런 말을 한 게 아니라는 것이다.

03. Expressions

1. you scared me to death

2. Now make a wish and blow out the candles

3. it's the thought that counts

04. Pattern Practice

1. 1 close your eyes and make a wish   2. 1 that counts

   2 listen to the music and dance to it   2 I want from you

   3 ready, (get) set and go   3 that I can give you

05. TOEIC 실전 문제 풀이

1. d

   [해석] 그 답이 틀렸다니 난 정말 놀랐다.

   [해설] a, b, c, d에 공통으로 나오는 surprise와 shocking은 단어의 의미상으로 둘 다 적합하다. 하지만 이 경우에는 -ed의 형태, 즉 수동 형태는 사람이 감정을 느낄 때 사용하는 것이기 때문에 d의 shocked가 정답이 된다.

2. c

   [해석] 이 영화 너무 감동적이야. 특히 Darcy가 Helen을 만나는 부분이 좋았어.

   [해설] a, b, c, d 모두 감정 표현의 의미를 담고 있기 때문에 의미상으로는 맞다. 하지만 사물이나 사람 등의 '타인'이 자신에게 감정을 느끼게 해 주는 능동적 주체가 될 때는 현재분사인 -ing으로 써야 한다. a와 d는 과거형이고 b는 동사원형이므로 오답이다.

3. d

   [해석] 이 촛불을 조심해서 들어주세요.

   [해설] 의미상으론 pull(밀다), touch(만지다), grab(쥐다), hold(잡고 있다) 모두 적절하다. 하지만 이 문장은 명령문이고, 명령문에서 동사는 원형으로 써야 한다. 따라서, d. hold가 의미상, 문법상 옳은 답이다.

07. Wrap Up

1. 1 you scared me to death

   2 now make a wish and blow out the candles

08. Comprehension Questions

1. d

   [해설] 국내에서만 사용 가능한 카드이기 때문에 해외에서는 사용이 안 된다.

2. b

   [해설] 해외 은행에서 새 계좌를 열어야지 출금이 가능하다.

09. Comprehension Questions

1. d

   [해설] 마이크는 슬리퍼 한 켤레를 사려고 한다.

2. b

   [해설] hottest item이란 가장 잘 팔리는 제품을 말한다.

10. Comprehension Questions

1. d

   [해설] grocery shopping에서는 식료품을 구매한다.

2. c

   [해설] 쿠폰이 어제 만료되었기에 마이크는 '오늘은 내 날이 아니다'라고 말했다.

11. Comprehension Questions

1. c

   [해설] 마이크는 4D의 특수 효과가 싫다고 말하고 있다.

2. b

   [해설] Matinee는 조조 영화인데 마이크가 조조할인을 받자고 말했다.

12. Comprehension Questions

1. b

   [해설] 유나는 마이크의 깜짝 생일 파티를 준비했다.

2. c

[해설] 유나는 선물보다도 성의 즉 마음이 가장 중요하다고 말하고 있다.

✳ **TOEIC 실전 문제 풀이**

1. d

[해석] 외국인도 해외 은행에서 계좌를 열 수 있다.

2. b

[해석] 참치 샌드위치 만들기는 매우 간단하다.

3. c

[해석] 요가 수업이 살을 빼는 데 바로 필요한 것일지도 모른다.

4. c

[해석] 나는 교수님을 만나 뵈려고 학교에 왔다.

5. b

[해석] 완전 싸다! 가격이 10달러 밖에 안 해.

6. c

[해석] 이 핑크색 립스틱이 오렌지 립스틱보다 더 인기가 많습니다.

7. c

[해석] 죄송하지만 저는 당신의 제안을 받아들일 수 없습니다.

8. c

[해석] 이 쿠폰의 만료일은 어제였습니다.

9. c

[해석] 너의 변명을 듣는 거 지겨워.

10. a

[해석] 다 한 뒤에 이메일 계정 종료하는 거 잊지마.

11. d

[해석] 나는 공포 영화보다 액션 영화를 선호한다.

12. c

[해석] 일찍 일어나는 새가 지렁이를 잡는다는 것도 모르니?

13. c

[해석] 나는 4D 영화관에서 의자가 흔들리고 물 뿌리는 거 싫어해.

14. b

[해석] 가로등이 희미하게 밝혀져 있다.

15. b

[해석] 널 잃어버린 줄 알았잖니. 간 떨어질 뻔했어!

16. d

[해석] 언어 학습자들에게는 많은 외국 경험을 추천한다.

17. c

[해석] 나는 영문학보다는 실용적인 영어를 배우고 싶다.

18. d

[해석] 나는 새 가위가 필요하다.

19. d

[해석] 난 25센트 4개와 10센트 5개가 있다. 총 1달러 50센트가 있다.

20. a

[해석] 이런 지루한 영화! 내 시간과 돈을 낭비했어.